PERFECTION

"*Oneing*" is an old English word that was used by Lady Julian of Norwich (1342–1416) to describe the encounter between God and the soul. The Center for Action and Contemplation proudly borrows the word to express the divine unity that stands behind all of the divisions, dichotomies, and dualisms in the world. We pray and publish with Jesus' words, "that all may be one" (John 17:21).

EDITOR:
Vanessa Guerin

PUBLISHER:
The Center for Action and Contemplation

ADVISORY BOARD:
David Benner
James Danaher
Ilia Delio, OSF
Sheryl Fullerton
Marion Küstenmacher

Design and Composition by Nelson Kane Design

Oneing

VOLUME 4 NO. 1

God's perfection is able to include imperfection;
what else could divine perfection be?
—Richard Rohr

ANY OF US could easily be confounded by and struggle with passages such as Matthew 5:48: "Therefore you are to be perfect, as your heavenly Father is perfect." In his article, "Perfection," the theme of this edition of *Oneing*, Timothy King shares his struggle with this passage and how, like many of us, he has caught himself "going down that slippery spiral of guilt, set off every time [he remembers he] will never attain perfection." However, once he examines and contemplates the passage and its context more carefully, he comes to a clearer understanding of what it reveals about *himself*.

The word "perfection," in both Hebrew and Greek, means completion or fulfillment, not faultless or flawless. In her article, "Perfection as Authenticity and Wholeness," Gigi Ross delves further into the etymology of the words perfection and completion, exploring the ways these words have been used historically, particularly in the Canonical and Gnostic Gospels. Her conclusion: We are called to be perfect or whole in the very way God empowers us to be—our perfectly *authentic* selves.

In "Perfection: A Problem and a Solution," Joseph Schmidt uses examples from the life of St. Thérèse of Lisieux to show how, by detaching herself from a lifelong struggle with willful thoughts and behaviors and "welcoming God's love into her imperfect and helpless heart," she could, by God's grace, learn to *willingly* practice "acts of mercy, forgiveness, and love."

Mirabai Starr experiences the sacred in all spiritual traditions. In "The Way of Imperfection: Teresa of Ávila and Our Blessed Humanness," she connects Teresa's teaching on detachment to that of Buddhism's Four Noble Truths, which "teach us that the cause of most of our suffering is the desire for things to be other than they are."

Gayle Scott struggled with just such a desire in India, where her idea of perfection paradoxically kept her from seeing perfection in each and every moment. In her compelling article, "The Unbearable Suchness of Holy Perfection," Gayle uses a quirky film character and her own life experience to illustrate the gifts and the shadows of the Enneagram Type One and the perfect world for which this type longs.

In his article, "The Trap of Perfectionism: Two Needed Vulnerabilities," Richard Rohr, also a Type One, shares at a very personal level—something he rarely does. He writes tenderly about his inner "little boy," making himself known and vulnerable, while also revealing the need, in his public persona, to present "a bulletproof exterior... whole, entire, and believable." What Richard has learned, and teaches, is that he "cannot protect some notion of perfection, nor [does he] need to promote [his] notion of perfection; only God defines and knows what perfection is."

None of us, with our limited understanding, can possibly "be perfect, as [our] heavenly Father is perfect." However, if we trust in God's merciful love, we learn, as Thérèse did, to welcome God into our experience and allow God to love perfectly through us—freeing us to detach from the need to control the outcome. James Alison beautifully articulates this at the end of his article, "Failure and Perfection":

> A sunset, a particular moment of unexpected delicacy in an operatic sextet, the tiniest turning towards love of an ungrateful child, a moment of contentment between partners in a publicly scorned relationship; these are, above all, glimpses of perfection when we have learned, in our failures, to let go of our grasp on what is good so that we can be surprised by the fierce tenderness of one who wants to overcome all our unrecognized hostility so as to crown us with glory.

I trust you will discover, through each of the articles in this edition of *Oneing*, the many glimpses of perfection we are given through experiences of failure and imperfection.

Vanessa Guerin,
Editor

CONTRIBUTORS

GIGI ROSS serves as the CAC's Administrative Coordinator for Education, working with the Living School and the online education programs. She also practices spiritual direction and is a member of the Threshold Choir, which sings in groups of two to four at the bedside of people who are dying. Her essay "Spiraling Into Trust" was published in the 2014 anthology *Embodied Spirits: Voices of Spiritual Directors of Color*. She looks forward to the publication of her essay on the contemplative foundations of social justice in the forthcoming sequel to *Embodied Spirits*. Gigi Ross can be contacted at giross@cac.org.

JOSEPH F. SCHMIDT is a De La Salle Christian Brother, a spiritual director, counselor, author, and retreat presenter. For many years he was on staff at The Sangre de Cristo Center for Spiritual Renewal, an international sabbatical center located in Santa Fe, New Mexico. The Center, which closed in 2012, offered a 100-day program for religious and priests on their spiritual journeys. Brother Joseph recently returned from five years of ministry in Kenya. He is the author of several books, including *Praying Our Experiences*, *Praying with Thérèse of Lisieux*, *Everything is Grace: The Life and Way of Thérèse of Lisieux*; and *Walking the Little Way*. Br. Joseph resides at La Salle University in Philadelphia and can be contacted by email at bjoeschmidt@gmail.com.

CHRISTIANNE SQUIRES, a spiritual director, was trained through the Audire School of Spiritual Direction in Central Florida and completed an MA in spiritual formation and leadership at Spring Arbor University. Focusing her master's thesis research on the intersection of digital connectivity and spiritual formation, Christianne has spent much of her vocational path exploring how Internet culture affects the soul and how it can be redeemed. She has offered workshops and webinars for Spiritual Directors International (SDI) titled "Spiritual Formation in a Google-ized World," "The Case for Spiritual Direction in the Technology Age," and "Using Technology Tools in Spiritual Direction: Is It for You?" In 2013,

Christianne was named one of SDI's New Contemplatives. She is the founder of Still Forming, an emerging online community that provides contemplative, formational space for pilgrims on the inner journey around the world, which she leads with her husband, Kirk. Christianne is a member of the Episcopal Church and lives in Winter Park, Florida. To learn more about Christianne Squires and Still Forming, visit http://www.stillforming.com/.

MIRABAI STARR lives in Taos, New Mexico and was a professor of Philosophy and World Religions at the University of New Mexico–Taos for twenty years. She speaks internationally about the teachings of the mystics, contemplative practice, and interspiritual dialogue. A certified bereavement counselor, Mirabai helps mourners harness the transformational power of grief and loss. An author of creative nonfiction and translator of sacred literature, Mirabai has received critical acclaim for her revolutionary translations of *Dark Night of the Soul* by St. John of the Cross, *The Interior Castle* and *The Book of My Life* by St. Teresa of Ávila, and *The Showings of Julian of Norwich*. Other books include *Mother of God Similar to Fire*; *God of Love: A Guide to the Heart of Judaism, Christianity and Islam*; the series *Contemplations, Prayers, and Living Wisdom*; and, most recently, *Caravan of No Despair: A Memoir of Loss and Transformation*. To learn more about Mirabai Starr, visit http://mirabaistarr.com/.

JACK JEZREEL holds a Master of Divinity degree from the University of Notre Dame and spent five years in a Catholic Worker community, providing support and housing for homeless men and women. Jack is the author of *Just*Faith, a formation program used in parishes across the US that prepares participants for the work of charity and justice. Over fifty thousand people in over one hundred and twenty Catholic dioceses have participated in the program. Jack is a popular and well-traveled speaker and teacher, and has been described as the "Johnny Appleseed" of the US Catholic church's social mission. Over the last thirty years, he has given more than one thousand lectures, presentations, and workshops dedicated to the Church's work of mercy and justice. Jack lives in Louisville, Kentucky with his wife, Maggie. They have three adult daughters, one son-in-law, and a ridiculously large garden. Jack Jezreel can be contacted by email at jack.jezreel@gmail.com.

JAMES ALISON is a Catholic theologian, priest, and author. He earned his doctorate in theology from the Jesuit Faculty in Brazil and lived with the Dominican Order between 1981 and 1995. James has lived in Mexico, Brazil, Bolivia, Chile, and the United States as well as his native England,

and he continues to travel as an itinerant lecturer and retreat leader. James is the author of numerous books, including *Knowing Jesus, Faith Beyond Resentment, On Being Liked, Undergoing God,* and *Broken Hearts and New Creations.* Many of his writings are available in numerous languages. James' most recent work is *Jesus the Forgiving Victim,* a program of induction into the Christian faith for adults, building upon René Girard's insight into desire. To learn more about James Alison and his work, visit http://www.forgivingvictim.com/ and http://www.jamesalison.co.uk/.

DAVID G. BENNER is an internationally known depth psychologist, author, and transformational coach. His passion and calling has been the understanding and facilitation of the unfolding of the self, associated with a journey of awakening. His educational background includes an Honors BA in psychology from McMaster University, an MA and PhD in clinical psychology from York University, and post-doctoral studies at the Chicago Institute of Psychoanalysis. He has authored or edited thirty books that have been translated into nineteen languages and has lectured on topics at the boundaries of psychology, spirituality, science, and philosophy in more than thirty-five countries. His most recent books include *Soulful Spirituality, Spirituality and the Awakening Self, Presence and Encounter,* and *Human Being and Becoming.* To learn more about David Benner, visit http://www.drdavidgbenner.ca/ and on Facebook and Twitter @DrDavidGBenner.

TIMOTHY KING is a graduate of North Park University with degrees in both theology and philosophy. He worked as a community organizer for the Industrial Areas Foundation on the South Side of Chicago and served for seven years at Sojourners in Washington, DC. Tim has been a guest on many radio shows and podcasts and has been interviewed for various print and online publications including ABC News, the BBC, CNN, TIME, *Christianity Today, The Christian Post,* and *The Daily Beast.* He currently lives and works at his family's farm in New Hampshire and enjoys thinking and writing about farming, food, and faith. To learn more about Timothy King, visit http://timothymichaelking.com/ or follow him on Twitter @tmking.

RICHARD ROHR is a Franciscan priest of the New Mexico Province and the Founding Director of the Center for Action and Contemplation (CAC) in Albuquerque, New Mexico. An internationally recognized author and spiritual leader, Fr. Richard teaches primarily on incarnational mysticism, non-dual consciousness, and contemplation, with a particular emphasis on how these affect the social justice issues of our time. Along with many recorded conferences, he is the author of numerous books, including *Eager to Love: The Alternative Way of Francis of Assisi* and *Dancing Standing Still: Healing the World from a Place of Prayer*. To learn more about Fr. Richard Rohr and the CAC, visit https://cac.org/richard-rohr/richard-rohr-ofm/.

Russ Hudson, one of the principal scholars and innovative thinkers in the Enneagram world today, is Executive Director of Enneagram Personality Types, Inc. and Co-Founder of The Enneagram Institute. He has been co-teaching the Enneagram Professional Training Programs since 1991, and is a Founding Director and former Vice President of the International Enneagram Association. He is co-author of several books on the Enneagram, including *The Wisdom of the Enneagram: The Complete Guide to Psychological and Spiritual Growth for the Nine Personality Types*. To learn more about Russ Hudson and the Enneagram Institute, visit http://www.enneagraminstitute.com/.

Gayle Scott is a member of the Senior Faculty for The Enneagram Institute and Director of the Enneagram Institute of Colorado. She is also a career veteran of both the Hollywood and Canadian film and television industries, and pioneered the use of the Enneagram as a tool for psychological character development for actors and screenwriters. Gayle teaches and consults internationally, and maintains an Integral Coaching practice. She works and lives high in the Rocky Mountains above Boulder, Colorado, surrounded by the sacred rhythms, blessings, and inspiration of the natural world. To learn more about Gayle Scott, visit https://www.enneagraminstitute.com/the-enneagram-institute-of-colorado/.

INTRODUCTION

IT IS QUITE UNFORTUNATE that the ideal of perfection has been applied to human beings. Strictly speaking, perfection can only be attributed to the Divine Self. Such a false goal has turned many religious people into pretenders or deniers—very often both. It has created people who, lacking compassion, have made impossible demands on themselves and others, resulting in a tendency toward superiority, impatience, dismissiveness, and negative/critical thinking.

In the secular sphere, it has manufactured artificial ledgers of perfection that have clearly changed from age to age, class to class, and culture to culture. Perfectionism discourages honest self-knowledge and basic humility, which are foundational to spiritual and psychological growth. It has made basic social tranquility a largely unachievable goal; grandiose people cannot create peace.

In the Christian world, perfectionism seems to have emanated from Jesus' teaching on loving our enemies—a seemingly impossible task. His exhortation has usually been translated as, "You shall be perfect as your heavenly Father is perfect" (found only in Matthew 5:48). So we set out alone, striving to be like God (perfect)—the very ideal against which we had been warned upon encountering the tree in Genesis 3:5. This, of course, greatly appealed to the grandiosity of the small self.

In effect, most Christian groups and individuals lowered the bar by emphasizing achievable goals usually associated with embodiment (attending church on Sunday, not committing adultery, not being a thief, not being gay, etc.)—goals for which we could take credit and "accomplish." These accomplishments only inflated our own self-image, not our love of God. Jesus never emphasized such things at all, because they could be achieved without any foundational love of God or love of neighbor—in other words, without basic conversion of either consciousness or identity. We could achieve this limited perfection through willpower, by "thinking correctly" about it, or by agreeing with a certain moral stance.

The moral goals of the Gospel can only be achieved through *surrender and participation*. These have often been ignored or minimized, even though they were clearly Jesus' major points (loving enemies, caring for the powerless, overlooking personal offenses, living simply, eschewing riches). We cannot take credit for these virtues; we can only thank God for them: "Not to us, O Lord, not to us, but to your name give glory" (Psalm 115:1).

The best we humans can do is to achieve a kind of perfection, in one small area—a craft or skill, or with some measurable talent—but never entirely. (Tiger Woods was perfect at golf until a more perfect Tiger Woods came along.) Only a very few win Olympic gold, silver, or bronze in the categories where they approach perfection. Most of us lose, give up, or do not even try to play the whole perfectionistic game. Thus many fall into small lives of "quiet desperation," deeply doubting their own souls and their divine identities inside their still-imperfect selves. No one has ever told them about the Gospel of freedom and mercy.

The search for a supposed perfection is the most common enemy of simple goodness. God just wants us to be humanly good, not perfect. Good people can always accept, and even love, imperfection. In fact, that is why they are usually called "good." Perfectionists live largely in their heads, creating their own criteria for some kind of supposed perfection. This very need for private perfection—apart from love of God or others—is surely the worst kind of imperfection: what we would call "sin." Yet it passes for heroism, idealism, and virtue in most individuals—until and unless they are liberated by the upsidedownness and insideoutness of the Gospel.

Have you ever noticed that values like forgiveness, tolerance, and mercy generally don't appeal to most cultures—or most individuals? For instance, observe the worlds of politics and most religious groups. They invariably hate and punish any kind of *vulnerability—which is simply owning and not hiding obvious imperfections.* True perfection, it seems, is usually well-hidden or disguised. It will always look like something else. It will often look like imperfection. The only real perfection of which humans are capable is to include, absorb, forgive, and transform all human imperfection. Humans are transformers much more than self-sufficient generators. Such is the character of a whole (and holy) human being.

Richard Rohr, OFM

This was his supreme philosophy,
    This his supreme desire,
    To inquire from both the wise and the simple,
    The perfect and the imperfect,
    The young and the old
    As to what perfection might be.

—Bonaventure on St. Francis[1]

Perfection as Authenticity and Wholeness

By Gigi Ross

IN MY SEARCH for a non-dual way to encounter perfection, a way that did not pit the perfect against the flawed, or even perfection against wholeness, I felt myself drawn to the word's etymology and to how perfection is understood in Christian non-dual texts and by Christian non-dual thinkers. *The New Oxford American Dictionary* traces the word "perfect" back to Middle English, with roots in an Old French word, *perfet*, which was formed from the Latin *perfectus*, meaning completed.[1] *Perfectus* is related to the verb *perficere*, formed from the prefix *per*, meaning both through and completely, and *facere*, meaning to do. Thus it seems that, while perfection first conveyed the idea of something done all the way through, completely, maybe even thoroughly, it did not originally entail comparison to a standard that had to be met. This earlier meaning of "perfect" can be found in a Christian understanding of non-dualism and transformation, but more about that later.

To complete my understanding of the original idea of perfection, I looked up the roots of "complete." This word can also be traced back to Old French and Latin. The Latin verb *complere* means to fill up, finish, fulfill.[2] To me, the Latin meaning points to ends, purpose, which brings me to one last word: teleology. Teleology, literally "the study of ends," explains phenomena based on the purpose they serve. The etymology of "perfect" and "complete" and the definition of "teleology" lead me to a meaning of perfection that has more to do with fulfillment of purpose than with a measure only saints can attain.

As alluded to above, this earlier meaning of the word "perfect" is more in line with the Biblical and early Christian sense than the current, generally accepted Western Christian interpretation. Other strands of Christianity have tended to remain closer to the original understanding. Lynn Bauman, in his translation of the Gospel of Philip, a non-dual Christian text thought to have been written near the beginning of the second century, explains that, for the author of the Gospel, the perfected human and the completed human are synonymous.[3] In *Christophany*, theologian Raimon Panikkar glosses the word "perfect," as used in the Roman Catholic collect for the Feast of the Transfiguration, this way: The collect "speaks of our 'perfect' (that is, complete) adoption."[4] The translator and the theologian are just two voices among many, pointing out a non-dual and non-guilt-inducing understanding of perfection that supports spiritual transformation.

The parallel between the early Christian understanding of perfection and the etymology of the English word doesn't end with the equivalence of perfection and completion. The Gospel of Philip, which scholars believe was written for the Syriac Church, alludes to One who "united Perfected Light with Sacred Spirit."[5] Lynn Bauman notes that perfected light is light that has been completed. The original Greek word in the Gospel is τέλειος (*teleios*), confirming that the idea of purpose, end, and teleology seems to be part of this Christian understanding of perfection as well.

For the author of the Gospel of Philip and others in this line of Christian non-dualism, perfection is not limited to divinity. Eastern Orthodox Christians speak of θέωσις (*theosis*), which is Greek

God empowers us to become our authentic selves, for that is who we are created to be.

for divinization. In the Gospel of Philip, Analogue 17, the author says those who are born of the Spirit are nourished with the grace flowing from God's mouth in order to make them complete. The fully realized human is the "Completed Human," as Lynn Bauman notes.[6] (We'll look at a reason for capitalizing this term later.) In making us complete, or fully realized, God grace-kisses us to perfection, fortifying us to become fully who we are created to be, so we can realize our purpose for living. Perfection, in this sense, consists of authenticity and wholeness.

God empowers us to become our authentic selves, for that is who we are created to be. The authentic person is the fully realized or completed person. We grow in perfection as we become who we are in God. Authenticity is essential to perfection, as described by Thomas Keating:

> Perfection does not consist in feeling perfect or being perfect, but in doing what we are supposed to do without noticing it: loving people without taking any credit. Just doing it.[7]

What I find most remarkable in Thomas Keating's description is the dearth of personal pronouns: only one. Perfection is not what we are; perfection is not even what *we* do; perfection is the loving done through us, which is one reason why it is not noticed and why no credit is taken. Instead, we are fulfilling our purpose, loving God and others, without trying, because, when we act authentically, we are not following a predetermined script or trying to live up to a certain standard. Consequently, our actions are "a response so great and wholehearted that we forget to be concerned about ourselves."[8]

We are not concerned about ourselves because we are not aware of ourselves as separate from our actions, motivations, or the situations in which we find ourselves. Living authentically or wholeheartedly, according to the purpose for which we are created—love—is living non-dually, completely, perfectly.

Another reason for not noticing or taking credit has to do with Lynn Bauman's capitalization of Completed Human. The Completed Human is not the completed individual. Maurice Friedman, writing about the Hasidic tradition, relates true wholeness to fulfilling the task for which we are created—Keating's "doing what we are supposed to do." Completing our purpose brings us into relationship with the rest of creation. "Our existence," Friedman continues, "does not take place *within* ourselves but in relationship to what is *not* ourselves."[9] We do not fully or completely or perfectly exist, and are not living authentically, until we move from existing within ourselves as individual humans, separated and isolated from other individuals, to being in relationship with all that we are not. This interdependent being-in-relationship is the person, the Human, who is completed or perfected. The separate individual relies on noticing and being noticed, taking credit and being praised or blamed, in order to confirm existence as an individual. A person living interdependently does not need evidence of personal existence, for, by authentically being in relationship, a person realizes wholeness.

Completed Human is capitalized to show the divinization of the person. Raimon Panikkar capitalized "Man" in *Christophany* for the same reason. "The complete Man is Man divinized; that unique being, athirst for the infinite, is not himself until he reaches his destiny...Man is more than his 'human' nature."[10] Here, too, perfection or completion is equated with authenticity ("is not himself") and wholeness ("until he reaches his destiny").

If we were reading Panikkar in Greek, his distinction between Man and man would be easier to understand because, in Greek, ἄνδρας (*andras*), "man," is used when distinguishing between a man and a woman, while ἄνθρωπος (*anthropos*), man or mankind, is not tied to a specific gender. *Anthropos* means human and was used by early Christians in the phrase Completed Human that we have been considering. Cynthia Bourgeault points to this meaning of *anthropos* in a presentation at the Center for Action and Contemplation conference *God As Us!* Referring to the Gospel of Thomas, Logion

114, she explains Jesus' response to Peter's complaint that, because she is a woman, Mary Magdalene should not be present with the male disciples who are receiving Jesus' secret teachings. After sarcastically responding that he would make her male if necessary, Jesus says, in a more serious tone, "I will transform her into a living Spirit because any woman changed in this way will enter the divine Realm."[11]

Cynthia Bourgeault explains that "living Spirit" is a translation of *anthropos*, the same word that has been translated as "fully realized human" and Completed Human. She notes that, for Jesus, living Spirit means someone who has integrated the opposites in an alchemical union.[12] In *The Meaning of Mary Magdalene*, she further observes that this is not just a union of opposites like male and female, or the psychological union of animus and anima, but a union on a cosmic scale, integrating within oneself infinite and finite, divine and human. This union "is accomplished through learning how to anchor one's being in that underlying unitive ground: the place of oneness before opposites arise."[13] She is describing contemplation. The one who lives from this ground is a fully realized, perfected human, authentic and whole. Everything belongs. Nothing is rejected.

We live in a realm where we taste separation more than union—at least, I know I do. That's why remaining grounded in oneness while living and moving in the realm of the many is a learning process, one we will not master or bring to completion or perfection until we are fully transformed. The author of the Gospel of Philip calls this transformation resurrection, equating the moment Jesus cried, "My

Perfection
is not what we are;
perfection is not even what we do;
perfection is the loving done
through us....

God, my God, why have you forsaken me?" with the moment of the complete separation of the divine realm from the human. When he was raised from the dead, these realms were reunited within him as before, "except now he came in a body that had been perfected."[14] Lynn Bauman explains the significance of Jesus' perfected body:

> Resurrection is the sign of the completed form where inner and outer, above and below are brought together into a new union which the newly completed body or form will hold together in unity. What we experience now is only a shadow (analogue or image) of what is true or real.[15]

At our most perfect, we are the Body of Christ, the Completed Human divinized, grounded in oneness that is the source of all opposites. As long as we are alive, however, we are not yet fully what we are becoming. We still have more deaths of separation, favoring one of the opposites over the other, and more resurrections, where we touch our authenticity and move closer to fulfilling the purpose for which we were created, until we reach the ultimate perfection: Holding the opposites as christs in Christ, rooted in oneness.   •

Perfection:

A Problem and a Solution

By Joseph F. Schmidt

A LITERAL MORAL understanding of Jesus' words, recorded in Matthew, "be perfect as your heavenly Father is perfect" (5:48), drops us into a deep psychological and spiritual pit on our spiritual path. We know we are not morally perfect and that we will never be perfect, as we commonly think of perfect: without fault, defect, or sin.

So what do we make of Jesus' words?

Some biblical scholars tell us that, in the text, "perfect" does not actually mean what we think, but means "complete," or "whole," or some similar notion. One recent interpretive translation (The Message) reads: "Live generously and graciously toward others, the way God lives toward you."

That translation fits Matthew's context much better, since "be perfect" concludes the thought that begins with "love your enemies," and includes the example of God's gifts of the sun and rain given to the bad and the good alike. God loves everyone, even those who do not love him: those who make themselves enemies of God.

Luke's parallel text (6:36), "be merciful (or compassionate) as your heavenly Father is merciful," translates more clearly what Jesus actually meant. Since God's perfection is mercy and forgiveness, even to the wicked, our perfection, like God's perfection, consists in forgiving and loving, even our enemies.

But we are left with the impression that we should "strive" to be perfect, at least to acquire the virtue of love. We quickly discover that striving—being iron-fisted and willful in our efforts to be merciful and loving—does not make us perfectly charitable; far from it. Willful, clenched-teeth striving is itself a spiritual trap.

We know that the presence of a willful, striving person does not make us feel God's perfection of love, forgiveness, and mercy. Rather, we feel as if we are being overpowered and coerced by a bully, even when the bully is giving us charity. Willful striving is not an attitude of love. It is a disguised form of self-centered ambition. It may be spiritual ambition, but it is egotistical ambition nonetheless.

Jesus' teaching, life, and death reveal that God's love, God's perfection, is not violent. Jesus' teaching is filled with mercy, his life with healing, and his death with forgiveness. He came that we might have life, and have it more abundantly.

We experience willfulness in others as violent and stifling of life and, when we notice willfulness in ourselves, we see that, yes, we are violent. Willfulness provides us with a noble-looking shovel, the shovel of violence, to dig ourselves out of the pit.

S o what to do? The good news is that we can only be lifted (loved) out of our helplessness by confidence in God's mercy. The better news is that our very frustration makes us ready to end our willful efforts and welcome God's love and lift. And the best news is that we have a contemporary saint who experienced this same helplessness and frustration, and showed us the little way of authentic Gospel perfection and love.

I would like to suggest that a solution to the "problem with perfection" might be found in the life and spirituality of St. Thérèse of Lisieux. Pope St. John Paul II said in the decree of 1997—on the hundredth anniversary of Thérèse's death—naming her a Doctor of the Church, "that the Spirit of God allowed her heart to reveal directly to the people of our time the *fundamental mystery*, the reality of the Gospel."[1] Thérèse, the pope said, is our contemporary, "a Teacher for the Church of our time."[2]

Thérèse of Lisieux, popularly known as The Little Flower, St. Thérèse of the Child Jesus, was keenly aware of her inadequacy and imperfections; specifically, she recognized the interconnection of her striving to be perfect with the violence of her willfulness.

Thérèse's spirituality was developmental and she came to discover that the essence of the Good News is that she did not need to be perfect. Rather, she was called to be willing (as opposed to willful) to welcome God's love into her imperfect and helpless heart and to share her heart with others. She willingly (not willfully) practiced acts of mercy, forgiveness, and love. Of course, she could not do this perfectly, but she did do it as best she could. Prayer and practice, patience and willingness became important aspects of Thérèse's little way—a spiritual path of love without any form of willfulness and violence.

IN HER WRITINGS, Thérèse revealed her own tendencies toward willfulness and violence, although she did not often use those words. Her mother described her as a stubborn, willful child. When Thérèse described her complete conversion, which happened just days before her fourteenth birthday, she named her contribution to the conversion, "my good will"—her willingness to be receptive to God's surprising and transforming grace. The miracle of her conversion relieved her of the unconscious violence she was doing to herself by her compulsive efforts to be perfect and pleasing. Her conversion was the gift of regaining her inner freedom from the domination and coercion of her excessive feelings. God gave her that gift in an instant—a gift she had struggled helplessly to willfully acquire during her prior ten years.

Thérèse also acknowledged her willfulness when she described her stubborn struggle to enter Carmel and to take her vows on dates she had decided—trying to bully God to accommodate her on her own terms.

In her autobiography, *Story of a Soul*, Thérèse referred explicitly to her own violence in at least two places. Early in her conventual

"...it is in my weakness that I glory, and I expect each day to discover new imperfections in myself."

—St. Thérèse of Lisieux

life, her primitive childhood feelings of separation from her mother surfaced, and she acknowledged her powerful, willful strivings to be connected to the convent superior. Recognizing how deeply she longed to be appreciated by a maternal figure, Thérèse confessed that she had "violent temptations to satisfy myself and to find a few crumbs of pleasure" by being close to Mother Gonzague.[3]

Thérèse also told the story about a sister toward whom she had hostile, violent feelings and was "tempted to answer her back in a disagreeable manner." Usually Thérèse did not show these feelings or act on them, but "was content with giving her my most friendly smile, and changing the subject of the conversation." Yet, Thérèse admitted, "Frequently, when I...had occasion to work with this sister, I used to run away like a deserter whenever my struggles became too violent."[4]

As Thérèse contemplated Jesus' words, "Love your enemies"—the ultimate touchstone to imitating God's perfection—she wondered how she could apply them to herself, living in the Carmelite convent with women committed to a life of prayer and love. Knowing the good intentions of the sisters, Thérèse said, "No doubt we don't have any enemies in Carmel."[5]

Thérèse believed that none of the sisters intended to be cruel or hostile and none were physically violent or thought of themselves as being an "enemy." But, to her reflection that "we don't have any enemies in Carmel," Thérèse added another truth with disarming honesty, "but there are feelings."[6] She could not deny that, in the presence of some harsh and contentious sisters, she felt as if she were in the presence of an enemy.

For Thérèse, the feelings of hostility were "natural feelings"—spontaneous and momentary. "Ah! What peace floods the soul," she remarked, "when she [the soul] rises above natural feelings."[7] But she also recognized that, if freely cultivated, these hostile natural feelings became poison, dripping violence into her heart.

From the experience of her childhood stubbornness and conversion, as well as from her years in Carmel, Thérèse knew the power of excessive natural feelings that moved her and other sisters to the violence of willfulness, harshness, disrespect, judgmentalism, and gossip. She also had experienced the inner peace that arose when she willingly accepted the embarrassment, the spiritual poverty, of having some of these feelings herself. "There is no joy comparable to that which the truly poor in spirit experience," she added to her comment about rising above natural feelings.[8]

Thérèse tells multiple stories of cultivating a willingness to be patient with herself and others—stories where she was not willfully striving to be perfect or to retaliate. She describes the thoughtless sister who splashed dirty laundry water in her face; the old, grouchy sister who frustrated Thérèse's best attempts to please her; the sister who sat behind her in chapel and drove her crazy with her clicking teeth; and the sister who became outraged and tried to bully her.

All of these stories—parables, really—describe how the perfection of the heavenly Father is manifested by loving the enemy in nonviolent, respectful, and merciful ways in life's ordinary events.

How did Thérèse rise above her natural feelings of willfulness, anger, retaliation, and violence? How did she maintain her sense of peace in the presence of the enemy?

She recognized that the key to her peace was her ability to accept these natural feelings as true, but not the whole truth, and so did not let them overpower her. She put her excessive feelings in the context of prayer, and thereby retained her inner freedom.

In prayer, she acknowledged that her heart was never perfectly free of her natural feelings. In practice, she followed, as best she could, a path that included responding to the irritating sisters—the enemy—with dispositions of compassion and creativity.

Thérèse responded compassionately to her enemies as she grew to recognize that the difficult sisters were burdened by their own imperfections and inner struggles. Thérèse saw similar burdens in herself and, in a spirit of solidarity and inner poverty, she responded compassionately—"suffering with"—the difficult sisters. She did not retaliate, but willingly responded to the sisters on their own terms.

She responded creatively to difficult sisters by not being attached to her own style or preferences. Her interactions contained elements of accommodation, originality, and flexibility. She was not rigid: To a sister who needed encouragement, she was affirming; to one she was expressive, to another reserved; to all, she was respectful. She smiled at "enemies" and performed other inconspicuous acts of charity. She did not demand that the sisters or the situations be perfect, and she relinquished any need to appear perfect herself.

ALTHOUGH RESERVED and deferential, Thérèse was not a doormat. Her stories reveal that she set boundaries, but did not bully. She was determined, but not predetermined, and did not build walls. She was passionate, but not inordinately so. When she could, she took initiative to heal problematic interactions among the sisters—all imperfectly.

Above all, she prayerfully bore her own imperfections. She was not self-condemning and she also extended creativity and compassion to herself. She was not impatient with herself for being impatient with others.

She followed her own advice, given to one sister: "If you are willing to bear serenely the pain of being displeasing to yourself, then you will be for Jesus a pleasant place of shelter."[9] She was willing to die daily in the painful poverty of knowing herself to be sinful and imperfect, and she accepted the inevitable sufferings of a nonviolent, loving person.

Thérèse's patient, pleasant manner and simple acts of kindness calmed the turbulent waters of community living. Her innate (sometimes compulsive) desire to please others, transformed by failure and prayer, contributed tenderness and empathy to her love for her sisters. One sister described her as an angel of peace for everybody. Another sister, who lived with Thérèse for nine years, thought she was not virtuous because virtue seemed to be effortless for her.

THÉRÈSE HAD NO formal theological or scriptural training; she never graduated from grade school. Her faith was founded on confidence in God's mercy, revealed especially in the Gospels. The New Testament became her only spiritual reading. Once she confided to a sister, as they stood together in the doorway of the convent library, that she thanked God she had not wasted her time reading any of the books. She said this, not from arrogance, but from an intuitive awareness that the spiritual literature of the time was tainted with Jansenism, Pelagianism, and perfectionism.

The common version of Jansenism at the time painted a distorted image of God as a tyrant, vengeful and punitive. Pelagianism popularly taught that, simply with willful efforts, holiness could be attained, and perfectionism took Matthew's text literally. Combined, these three mistakes reduced Christianity to an impossible moralistic discipline. Thérèse rightly understood the Good News to be a welcoming faith-relationship with Christ, who loved her and empowered her to live out that love in her own life. In the final years of her life, Thérèse said that, if "her" love was really Gospel love, it would be Jesus Christ's love, and so would be, of course, without violence.

The mistaken spirituality of Thérèse's time contaminated the spirituality of her Carmelite community and most of the Church. In the decree making Thérèse a Doctor, John Paul II wrote that

"God does not demand great acts from us, but only surrender and gratitude."

—St. Thérèse of Lisieux

"She helped to heal souls of the rigors and fears of Jansenism."[10] She clearly did that and, further, she helped heal souls of Pelagianism and perfectionism as well—attitudes that had prompted some of the well-intentioned sisters to willful and violent efforts to correct her, as well as to attain their own perfection.

❧

THE PARABLE of the Pharisee and the publican became one of Thérèse's favorite parables (Luke 18:9–14). In imitation of the publican, she embraced her sinfulness and was willing to "bear with myself, such as I am with all my imperfections."[11] She surrendered herself to God's mercy, as did the publican, with confidence that, "What pleases God is that He sees me loving my littleness and my [inner] poverty, the blind hope that I have in His mercy."[12] "I am not disturbed at seeing myself weakness itself," she wrote without violent self-condemnation; "on the contrary, it is in my weakness that I glory, and I expect each day to discover new imperfections in myself."[13] And, like the publican, she was not violent to others through blame or condemnation.

In prayer, she responded to her own imperfections—"the enemy" within—and to the imperfections of the sisters—"the enemy" outside—according to the response of the publican. She wrote: "The remembrance of my faults humbles me, draws me never to depend on my strength, which is only weakness, but this remembrance speaks to me of [God's] mercy and love even more."[14]

In prayer, remembering her imperfections, she yielded to God's embrace. She could not climb the rough stairway of perfection; God's arms would lift her.

Thérèse joined her spirit of self-surrender to God's mercy with a spirit of gratitude—gratefulness not just for "things" in her life, but for existence and life itself. She found peace in the awareness that "God does not demand great acts from us, but only surrender and gratitude."[15] The dispositions of inner freedom, willingness, compassion, creativity, self-surrender, and gratitude became the heart-qualities that guided Thérèse on the path of love—a love that harbored no violence.

THÉRÈSE SHIFTED her focus more and more from attaining perfection or acquiring holiness to the attitude of the publican: She let God's mercy *be* her perfection, her holiness. "I desire, in a word, to be a saint," she prayed, "but I feel my helplessness and I beg you—Oh my God!—to be Yourself my Sanctity!"[16] "Jesus, draw me into the flames of your love," she wrote. "Unite me so closely with you that you live and act in me."[17]

These prayerful sentiments expressed her solution to the problem of perfection. She had arrived at a complete reversal of her original idea of what it means to be on the path of Gospel holiness. Gospel holiness had less to do with willful striving for the perfection of moral achievements or the elimination of defects, and more to do with receiving God's compassion and forgiveness; with willingly deepening her union with God in Christ; with letting God's will totally trump her willfulness; and with not retaliating, even to those whom she perceived as "the enemy." Gospel perfection consisted in surrendering even her ambition to love God perfectly to an attitude of letting her love of God consist in letting God love her and willingly sharing love with others in simple acts of charity. Christian perfection, Thérèse recognized, consisted in receiving God's mercy and being empowered by God's love to love, even "the enemy," without violence of any kind.

Thérèse called her way "new," and even today it is a contemporary understanding of authentic Gospel holiness, by which she helps to bring healing to the Church and to this world, so violent in our day. •

The Messiness of Community:

An Invitation to Intimacy, Truth-Telling, and Grace

By Christianne Squires

IN 1975, Henri Nouwen published a book called *Reaching Out* in which he explored the movements from loneliness to solitude, from hostility to hospitality, and from illusion to prayer in the spiritual life. Early in the book, he shares an excerpt of a journal entry he penned during a trip to New York City, which began with this observation: "Sitting in the subway, I am surrounded by silent people hidden behind their newspapers or staring away in the world of their own fantasies. Nobody speaks with a stranger, and a patrolling policeman keeps reminding me that people are not out to help each other."[1]

Nouwen wrote these words over forty years ago and yet he could have written them today. Who is not familiar with this scene on the subway? Transpose it to any other public place—the airport, the doctor's office, the car wash, or any coffee shop—and replace the newspaper with a smartphone, and you have the very same scene. What's more, our distrust of our neighbors has increased, as catastrophic events like 9/11 dispose us toward perpetual suspicion and fear. The proliferation of information online has increased our awareness of ongoing danger and evil in the world while increasing our susceptibility to personal privacy violations. More than ever, we seem wired to distrust community and protect ourselves.

Yet this posture of "self first" is nothing new. From the beginning of the Scriptures through the end of its pages, we see this truth reflected back to us. Adam betrayed Eve in his moment of shame, telling God, "The woman whom you gave to be with me, she gave me fruit from the tree, and I ate" (Genesis 3:12). Cain slew Abel, his brother, in a fit of jealousy. In fear for his life, Abraham passed off his wife, Sarah, as a sister. Joseph's brothers, incensed by his prophetic dreams and his role as their father's favorite, threw him into a pit and then sold him into slavery. Moses attempted to right an injustice he witnessed among his Hebrew kin by killing an Egyptian and then fled when confronted with what he'd done. Years later, when leading the Israelites to the Promised Land, he contended almost continually with their grumbling, complaining, and blame. David's brothers mocked him for being a shepherd boy, and Saul pursued him years later with murderous intent.

Protagonists in the New Testament fare no better. The disciples argued among themselves about which of them was greatest, while James and John approached Jesus to seek seats at his right hand, drawing the indignation of the other ten. Judas betrayed not only Jesus but also the rest of the Twelve with his traitorous act. Jesus' three closest friends could not watch for one hour with him in his time of need—and then all the disciples fled. Saul persecuted the church before asking to be received into their ranks. Ananias and

Intimacy with God leads us toward community.

Sapphira lied to their community of trust. Paul and Barnabus broke fellowship in their ministry travels. And, in the book of Revelation, we see the Son of Man reproaching the seven churches for the ways they failed to walk justly and love mercy in their dealings with God, each other, and the world.

In such a broken system, is it any wonder we lack the trust true community requires? Is it so hard to believe we would wander our own way, content to rely upon ourselves and the private life with God we can cultivate alone? Should it surprise us that we choose to live defended, protected lives, armored in isolation?

GOD'S DESIGN

IT IS, INDEED, understandable that we should live this way, distrusting community. And yet that is not God's way. From the beginning, God declared it was not good for man to be alone (Genesis 2:18). In fact, his first words to the first man and woman, after blessing their existence, was, "Be fruitful and multiply, and fill the earth" (Genesis 1:28). He commanded them toward an experience of life in community.

It doesn't end there. God called Abraham to father many nations. He birthed Israel through the renaming of Jacob. He named Moses their leader and then led them as a people. As Richard Foster writes, "God led the children of Israel out of bondage *as a people*. Everyone saw the cloud and fiery pillar. They were not a gathering of individuals who happened to be going in the same direction; they were a people under the theocratic rule of God."[2]

Jesus, in his life of ministry, chose the Twelve and then extended his work through the seventy. He drew three—Peter, James, and John—especially close. And then, in the coming of the Holy Spirit, we see the birth of the church, where "all who believed were together and had all things in common.… Day by day, as they spent much time together in the temple, they broke bread at home and ate their food with glad and generous hearts, praising God and having the goodwill of the people" (Acts 2:44–47). Thousands were added to their number as they lived this way together. And, finally, through the beloved disciple John, we are given a vision of the end of days, of a city that exists in perpetual adoration of God and in harmony with itself (Revelation 21–22).

OUR RESPONSE

THROUGH THE DEMONSTRATION of the Scriptures, then, we see we are meant for community. But how do we live this way? How do we bridge the gap between God's design and our inherent self-reliance and suspicious disposition toward one another? Is there any hope for such a life to exist among us?

I contend that there is—and, furthermore, that attending to this aspect of our lives is an essential component of Christian spiritual formation. To get to a place of living healthfully in community, we find that three factors are key: 1) an intimate relationship with God, 2) a receptivity to truth-telling, and 3) an openness to the messy reality of our shared humanity. Each of these three factors is a necessary component of the healthful formation God intends for us in our human experience. Let's explore each of them in turn.

-1-

AN INTIMATE RELATIONSHIP WITH GOD

IT MAY BE surprising to hear that our life in community begins with our personal, intimate relationship with God, but it does. Here again, we are guided by the examples found in Scripture. We're told Moses spoke to God as one speaks with a friend. Abraham, too, spoke directly with the God of the universe. Joseph communed with God in dreams. David freely penned psalms declaring his heart's praises and protestations. The major and minor prophets—Isaiah, Jeremiah, Ezekiel, Hosea, and all the rest—knew an intimacy with God that allowed ample room for confessions, arguments, and tears. Jesus maintained the perfection of intimacy with the Father, declaring himself unable to speak or do anything apart from the Father's direction. Peter spoke with boldness and received a friendship with Jesus that endured and absorbed all his missteps. John leaned upon Jesus' breast. Paul encountered the resurrected Christ in a burst of light that blinded him and propelled him into a days-long form of solitude with God.

It is perhaps fitting for us to notice that each one of these individuals, from a place of intimacy, went forth to lead communities. From the moment God spoke the covenant over him, Abraham gathered his family and headed to Canaan. From the back-and-forth conversation with God that conveyed his unexpected calling, Moses led Israel out of Egypt and toward the Promised Land. David reigned as an unlikely but beloved king of a nation. The prophets proclaimed the truth of God to the people of Israel. Peter became the rock of the church. John wrote to the "little children…fathers…[and] young people" he led into the truths of God (1 John 2:12–13). Paul founded numerous first-century churches. And Jesus led the disciples, as well as the crowds that followed him, through all the nearby towns and villages. Intimacy with God leads us toward community, indeed; it cannot help but do so.

Yet the opposite is also true. When Adam and Eve broke communion with God, following a path other than the one prescribed for them, it led to brokenness between themselves, as Adam blamed Eve and Eve blamed the serpent and they covered themselves with leaves to hide their shame. When David departed from the way he ought to have gone, taking Bathsheba as his own though she was married to another man, the result was intrigue upon intrigue that eventually led to murder. In the New Testament, when Saul trusted his own righteousness, this led to the persecution and killing of countless believers. Furthermore, his later encounter with the risen Christ thrust him back toward community, as he sought to be forgiven and folded in among their number. In all this, we see that intimacy with God grounds our lives and propels us toward community, while a lack of intimacy with God leads us to broken fellowship with our fellow human beings.

-2-
A RECEPTIVITY TO TRUTH-TELLING

TRUTH-TELLING plays an important role in community life as well, just as it affects our intimacy with God. We see in the life of David, for example, that it was the confrontation of Nathan the prophet—and David's receptivity to that confrontation—that restored his soul. Once David confessed, Nathan told him the Lord had put away his sin so he would not die.

Truth-telling preserves Abraham's soul in relationship, when King Abimelech confronts him about the lie he told concerning Sarah, saying, "What have you done to us? How have I sinned against you, that you have brought such great guilt on me and my kingdom? You have done things to me that ought not to be done.... What were you thinking, that you did this thing?" (Genesis 20:9–10). Abraham confesses, and this not only leads to King Abimelech giving him sheep, servants, oxen, and land, but also to God hearing the prayer of Abraham to grant children to the king. We begin to see that truth-telling can lead to confession that is restorative on both a human and a divine level.

Jesus provides us with a similar model for truth-telling in relationship. Yes, there is the clear reality that he came to speak the truth to those he met and taught, and to offer himself as Truth incarnate in all he did. But in his closest relationships, he also demonstrated an openness to self-disclosing vulnerability that manifested itself through truth-telling. He voiced his discouragement at their lack of understanding and his disappointment in the ways they let him down—most notably when they fell asleep in the garden after he'd asked them to watch and pray with him. In this, he models for us that speaking the truth of our experience in relationship, even when it means speaking hard things, is a necessary part of our health in community.

On the other hand, we see that those who chose *not* to live in truth faced dire consequences. When Moses could not face the confrontation of his murderous act against the Egyptian, he fled the scene and tended sheep in the wilderness for forty years. (Thankfully, when God met him many years later at the burning bush, Moses had learned how to better enter into difficult conversations, as he fired one question after another at this God, who took the time to answer every single one.) We also see that Ananias and Sapphira, in choosing to lie about their offering to the community, died on the spot. And from Paul's letters, we learn that those who taught any gospel other than the true gospel were to be cast out of their communities. Living in truth and speaking truth to one another comprise essential pieces of communal living.

-3-

AN OPENNESS TO OUR MESSY HUMANITY

WHILE TRUTH-TELLING is a necessary component of God's intention for community, it is the forgiving grace we carry toward each other's messy humanity that makes such truth-telling

We need each other to grow into the people we're meant to be.

redemptive and restorative rather than destructive. As Henry Cloud has been known to say, "In the same way Truth (without grace) can be called Judgment, Grace (without truth) can be named License."[3] We need both grace and truth to live in the fullness of God's intention for us, just as Jesus, "full of grace and truth" (John 1:14), modeled for us by coming to this earth—speaking truth and yet coming near, descending into a world of complexity and struggle to be with us in it.

Being God incarnate, his was a model for relationship that existed from the beginning. When God set this world and its system in motion, he moved toward Adam and Eve, creating a model for relationship that depended on their participation for its fulfillment. When they failed to live up to their side of equation, that carried consequences (truth)—and yet God could not help but move toward humanity again (grace), this time approaching Noah and setting another system in motion. Later still, he moved toward Abraham, then Moses, then Israel, again and again, through its many prophets.

In our need to learn relationship, then, we learn from the model of our God, who moves toward us in our frailty, speaking truth and yet never failing to come back, again and again, when we fail to live up to it. We see this grace and truth extended to Peter on the beachside at breakfast—the invitation to feed Christ's sheep, even after he'd denied Christ three times before Christ died. And the early church continued this example. When conflict arose among them, as in the feeding of the widows, they assembled, discussed, and created a fitting plan for moving forward. When Paul came among the community of believers after his conversion, seeking to become part of their number, those who knew his past spoke their fear. Yet Barnabus proved instrumental in helping bridge the divide between persecutor and persecuted, dousing their difficult shared history with grace. When Paul observed Peter failing to abide by the eating standards he knew Christ's freedom made possible, he spoke to Peter in truth and then continued in fellowship with him.

The message in all of this is the reality of our shared humanity. Will we live with each other in the truth of this reality? Will we let one another be human, offering each other grace even as we "provoke one another to love and good deeds" (Hebrews 10:24) by speaking the truth in love? It ought to be so, as it is our shared humanity—messy though it is—that puts us on equal footing with one another before God. We are humans, all of us, each with blind spots and growing edges. We need each other to grow into the people we're meant to be. •

The Way of Imperfection:

Teresa of Ávila and Our Blessed Humanness

By Mirabai Starr

T HE WAY OF PERFECTION is the one book by my beloved Teresa of Ávila that I have stubbornly refused to translate. In part, it's the very title that has put me off. I have spent the second half of my life recovering from the perfectionism to which I subjected myself during the first half. Much of my focus in teaching has been on trying to help people, mainly women, release the burden of not-enough-ness and too-much-ness. *The Way* is a rather strident manual on living in spiritual community, and contains detailed directives and harsh exhortations for religious aspirants.

Most of the rest of Teresa's body of work resonates with me. Her other books are more mystical, poetic, rapturous. Translating *The Interior Castle* was a privilege, as I followed Teresa's sandal tracks through the landscape of the soul into the arms of the mystery. After the theological complexity of the *Castle*, it felt like dessert to translate *The Book of My Life*, in which my sixteenth-century sister gleefully recounts her youthful misadventures. But whenever I would pick up *The Way of Perfection*, I'd find myself setting it down again with a sigh. I want to help people *be with what is* and embrace it as sacred, not cajole them into praying harder, mortifying themselves, and rejecting personal relationships, which is what *La Madre* advocates in this bossy treatise on religious life.

But recently, as I finally began to explore the text, some of the knots I first perceived untied themselves, revealing an array of treasures I recognize as having direct value in navigating spiritual life as a contemporary seeker of Truth. I would like to share a few of these hidden pearls and explore how they might be not only relevant, but vital to our own journey.

CONTEMPLATIVE LIFE

FIRST I MUST come clean: I am an interspiritual being. That is, I say *yes* to the presence of the sacred wherever I find it: in the Eastern traditions and in the monotheistic faiths, in nature and in the quiet depths of the formless. And so, in this exploration of Teresa's *Way*, you will find reference to multiple religious frameworks.

One of the things I love about Hinduism is its inclusiveness. The Four Yogas, for example (*Jnana, Bhakti, Karma,* and *Raja*), honor the temperamental differences between spiritual seekers: Some are more philosophical, while others are more devotional; some tend to be active and others are naturally meditative. Teresa too makes it clear that the spiritual journey is different for everybody and no one map will lead us all home. While her work emphasizes silent prayer, she reminds us that the path of the contemplative is not for everyone. "St. Martha was holy, though they don't set her down as a contemplative," Teresa writes. "Well, what more would you want than to get to be like this blessed woman, who deserved to have Christ Our Lord so often in her house, and to give him food and serve him ...?" Then, she sensibly suggests, "If we are to set ourselves up as inebriated, like the Magdalen, there won't be anyone to give the Celestial Guest something to eat."[1]

We will not all be inclined to turn inward and rest in the mystery. Many of us find ourselves more at home engaged in the world, offering up the fruits of our actions to God. This is not a problem, Teresa says. Be true to your own essence, because this is what the Beloved has instilled in your soul. Nevertheless, she does advocate that all of us who walk a spiritual road should cultivate some form of contemplative practice, allowing this "loving conversation with God" to be the garden from which our fullest humanity flowers and ripens, whether in silence and stillness or in the messy midst of community—or, for many of us, in some combination of these.

LOVE

"Love the Lord your God with all your heart and with all your soul and with all your strength," Jesus said, "and love your neighbor as yourself" (Mark 12:30–31).This is the core of Teresa's understanding of the inner life and its outer expression. The love that is rooted in God germinates in community and spreads through creation.

Devotion has picked up a negative connotation in the contemporary spiritual scene. Those who favor a non-dual approach sometimes mistakenly conclude that a devotional orientation, with its emphasis on love-longing, implies a false sense of separation and that the more elevated and mature spiritual state is one in which we affirm that we are already one with God, and with all that is.

Through their own example, mystics like Teresa teach us that, when we allow our hearts to break open with longing, that for which we yearn comes pouring into the shattered container, filling and healing us, and dissolves all boundaries between lover and Beloved. The resulting unitive experience plunges us into a non-dual state of consciousness, from which we emerge forever (even if subtly) changed. At their mystical heart, all the world's religions celebrate this dance between separation and union, longing and return. When we pour

Be true to your own essence, because this is what the Beloved has instilled in your soul.

the wine on *Shabbat*, the Jewish Sabbath, the empty *kiddush* cup represents the heart that cries out for God, and the wine symbolizes God's instantaneous response as he fills our waiting vessel with love.

A natural outflow of the intimacy we taste in deep states of prayer and meditation is an inclination to see the face of the Holy One reflected in all our relationships. When we have truly fallen in love with the Divine, we can no longer view individual human beings, animals, or the earth herself as "other." We recognize the interconnectedness of all that is, not as an intellectual belief, but as a lived experience, one that rises from loving God with all our heart and all our soul and all our might.

DETACHMENT

THE IMPORTANCE of extricating ourselves from attachment seems to be a universal tenet throughout the world's great wisdom traditions. The Four Noble Truths of Buddhism teach us that the cause of most of our suffering is the desire for things to be other than they are, and that, if we wish to be happy, we should work on unclenching our fist. Clinging to what makes us feel good and pushing away uncomfortable things robs us of the opportunity to expand the capacity of our beings to embody the full spectrum of the human condition. Lamenting the past and projecting into the future takes us away from the present moment, which is real and complete.

Although Teresa is very firm in *The Way of Perfection* about the need to cultivate interior poverty—what she calls *la vida nonada*, "the nothing life"—she also understood that there are some attachments that connect us to the Divine, rather than cut us off from the Divine. In one of many stories about Teresa and her protégé, John of the Cross, John suggests that Teresa may be overly fond of the statues of saints and images of Jesus she has collected in her cell, and so she takes them all away—and then feels utterly bereft. Soon after, Teresa has a vision of Christ in which he tells her that anything that reminds her of him is a good thing, so she puts them all back.

Teresa of Ávila suffered from a variety of chronic illnesses throughout her life. In the tradition of many great Christian mystics, from Hildegard of Bingen and Julian of Norwich to Thérèse of Lisieux and Edith Stein, Teresa endeavored to engage her physical suffering as an opportunity to participate in the Passion of her beloved Christ, and she instructed her spiritual sisters to do the same. Rather than complain about every little ache and pain, Teresa chides us, we may instead meet these challenges with gratitude and keep our discomfort to ourselves. In this way, we allow such experiences to work their alchemy inside us, transmuting our base substance into something golden.

La Madre makes exceptions, of course, for serious health conditions, which we should not ignore. False detachment can be more dangerous than over-indulgence, because it is predicated on pride masquerading as humility, and it can do grave harm. Teresa was also suspicious of self-mortification. Too much penance—in the form of fasting, isolation, or refusal to stand up for ourselves when wrongfully accused—can simply be a more insidious form of attachment. In such cases, Teresa would send her nuns to bed with a bowl of soup. Beware of confusing self-care with self-indulgence. Find healthy and balanced ways to nurture the vessel you are so that you can create a welcoming space for the Holy One to abide in you.

PRAYER

TERESA TEACHES THAT there are three stages of prayer, and that contemplative life is a combination of discipline and grace. In cultivating contemplative practice, we create an environment in which increasing degrees of intimacy with the Holy One may unfold within us.

Teresa names the first stage the Prayer of Recollection. When we make the effort to set aside time to be still and turn inward, we gather all our faculties to a single point of concentration and invite the presence of the sacred to enter us. "However quietly we speak, he is so near that he will hear us," Teresa writes in *The Way of Perfection*. "We need no wings to go in search of him, but have only to find a place where we can be alone and look upon him, present within us."[2] In this state, we may find that what the Buddhists call "monkey mind" continues to chatter for a while, but gradually things settle down and a kind of spaciousness begins to open between the thoughts, and that's where the Holy One slips in to sit beside us.

The Prayer of Recollection involves our active participation. It requires discipline, concentration, and a willingness to endure both mental turmoil and spiritual aridity. It is an act of purification; by

The love that is rooted in God germinates in community and spreads through creation.

scouring the vessel of our souls with the practice of prayer, we empty ourselves so that the Beloved may fill us.

At that point, we may enter the Prayer of Quiet. Now that the labor of recollection has cleansed us, we are ready to receive the infusion of divine light. This is a state of grace. While the Prayer of Recollection is a matter of personal intention, the Prayer of Quiet is a gift. Once we have gathered our senses and intellect, a feeling of deep peace and quietude may wash over us like a warm wave. This is an exceedingly delicate experience. It is sweet and restful. It is timeless. We cannot manufacture or manipulate this stage of prayer. We can only make ourselves ready to receive it when it comes and, in the words of the late meditation teacher Stephen Levine, we "hold on tightly and let go lightly."[3]

The Prayer of Quiet is not a state of complete absorption—what is known as *samadhi* in the Eastern traditions. The mind may wander, but it doesn't matter. The soul is aware of the love story unfolding deep inside her, and that's where the focus is. Recognition of separation lingers, coupled with a feeling of awe to be in the presence of the Holy. We may be filled with a sense of longing for a deeper connection with that which transcends our individuality, but we remain in a dualistic relationship with the ultimate source of love.

In Teresa's final stage, the Prayer of Union, any sense of an individualized self slips away. The soul merges with the Divine, like a drop of water into the boundless sea. The Beloved, who, as it turns out, has longed for the lover as fervently as she has desired him, makes her one with him. The Prayer of Union is usually fleeting, but its impact endures. Each time God blesses us with these unitive experiences, we are forever transformed. We are likely to still bumble through the human condition, behaving unskillfully at times and with more grace at others, but with each taste of union we identify a little less with the individual personality and more with our essential unity with the Divine. We are less likely to take passing circumstances as seriously as we used to. Our values shift from acquiring security to serving the One through being of service in the world.

The contemplative life is not a matter of achieving some artificial state of perfection available only to the spiritual elite, who glide past the obstacles that throw off the rest of us. It is a matter of being so fully present to the moment that we cannot help but catch a glimpse of God in all that is. "Which of my blessings," the Holy One asks in the Qur'an, "will you deny?"[3]

Teresa of Ávila is one of the great advocates and models of the power of simply sitting for a few minutes each day in silence and stillness, and striking up a conversation with the One who is waiting to love us unconditionally, the One who will never leave us, the One who is not different from the essence of who we truly are. •

To Love Without Exception

By Jack Jezreel

MY FRIEND Kyle Kramer, who serves as Executive Director of the Passionist Earth & Spirit Center in Louisville, Kentucky and who, like me, has spent some time as a farmer, recently wrote a short piece on the practice of contemplation, likening it to the agricultural practice of frost seeding. Frost seeding involves broadcasting seed at the start of winter and, instead of plowing and drilling, relying on the slow, steady, daily freezing, thawing, and melting of ice, snow, and ground to draw the seed down into the soil. Then, lo and behold, a few months later there is a spring crop!

He goes on to suggest that contemplation, as difficult as it can sometimes be, nevertheless has this steady, slow, reliable effect on our selves. Even as we might be frustrated with our seemingly feckless efforts, that effort, multiplied by time and attention, yields a crop. I love and trust the image of slow, deliberate change.

I use this image as an opening tribute to the work of Richard Rohr and the profound effect it has had on my life and the lives of many, many others. I was first introduced to Richard at a charismatic renewal conference in Tampa, Florida in the early 1980s. He was one of two keynote speakers; the other was a good-humored nun named Mother Angelica (as you may know, they would later go in very different spiritual directions). Here was this twenty-something priest (who looked like he was fifteen!) speaking in a way that was fresh, intelligent, provocative, and enthusing. Ever since that time, I've been one of Richard's groupies, going to his conferences and workshops, reading his books, and listening to his recordings.

The effect, over the thirty-five years that I have been mentored by Richard, is that now, when I read his writing, I no longer say, "Wow!" I say, "Of course." The frost seeding and the slow but steady (albeit imperfect) integration of Richard's teaching in my heart, mind, soul, and feet has nourished and steered me. I would insist that I am a more faithful, freer, more compassionate, happier man than I would have been without the teaching and witness of Richard Rohr. I hope that sounds like the highest compliment.

I NSPIRED BY RICHARD's teaching, the witness of Dorothy Day, and the writing of the Latin American liberation theologians, I have spent the last thirty years as an educator, trying to make clear the link between the critical insights of a mature spirituality and the work of compassion and justice. (I am guessing this resonates with those connected to an organization called the "Center for Action and Contemplation.") I would like to think that my work, as inspired as it has been by Richard, has reinforced and complemented Richard's insights by emphasizing more of the action/compassion part of the relationship. So, what I have to offer here might add some "variations on the original theme" and possibly some generative tension.

In Richard's Introduction, he rightly observes the misappropriation of Matthew 5:48 ("You shall be perfect as your heavenly Father is perfect"). This is *not* an exhortation to some kind of ambiguous and impossible life lived *without error*; it *is*, however, a very challenging exhortation to love *without exception*. In other words, this "perfect" language is intended as a description of how love is to be offered—that is, without exceptions. To exclude anyone is to love imperfectly. In effect, this very compelling passage proclaims that the nature of love and the nature of God—and the path to wholeness and holiness—is that they are necessarily and constitutionally inclusive of all.

To exclude anyone is to love imperfectly.

In some notes I took almost thirty years ago at one of Richard's lectures, I wrote down a phrase that Richard spoke with his usual eloquent impact: that the import of this passage from Matthew's Gospel was that "you either love the whole or you only prefer the parts; you either love everyone or you don't love anyone—you just prefer them, based on a set of characteristics that you find acceptable." The insight is fabulously provocative and helpful. It mimics Dorothy Day's challenge—we really only love God as much as we love the person we love the least. Richard's and Dorothy's similar insights are at once both spiritually revelatory and practically instructive, as good teaching should be.

The message is that we are either a people who love, embrace, and enter into a caring posture with our family, friends, neighbors, strangers, and even enemies (real or imagined) *or* we will spend our lives mercilessly trying to define who is lovable and who is not, who is worthy and who is not, who deserves my attention and who does not. Inevitably, we will end up loving people who look like us, think like us, and pledge allegiance to the same flag—and we will exclude the rest. In this truly useless pursuit, we will separate ourselves from God (through tribal worship), from the world's good (by avoiding healing and restoration), and from our very souls (through self-preoccupation with ego).

Matthew 5:43–48, combined with Matthew 25:31–46 ("I was hungry and you gave me food"), suggests that a critical touchstone and measure for the true disciple is the embrace of and care for all, evidenced by relationship, especially with those who are typically "the exceptions and the excluded," namely the poor, the outcast, the stranger, the enemy, the one who inconveniently presses upon my time, attention, and conscience. In Catholic social teaching, this moral and spiritual beckon is called the "preferential option for the poor and vulnerable."

Personal transformation and social transformation are one piece.

In effect, the wisdom of Jesus describes the powerful, but often neglected, bridge between spiritual insight and social action/real compassion. In fact, the wisdom of Jesus seems to suggest that the link is even more intimate than a bridge; it is the collapse of the two categories altogether. The separation of spirituality from action is a false one. In other words, we are not called to do spiritual practices—prayer, study, meditation, retreat, ritual—and then make our way, now inspired, to the work of mercy and justice. In fact, it might be argued that, if anything, it's just the reverse: Love those who struggle with poverty and suffer abandonment and the effect is that we will find ourselves on a path that leads to maturity, prayer, wisdom, and Christ-likeness. If, however, we choose to avoid engagement and community with those who suffer, we will certainly live an incomplete life, including an incomplete spiritual life.

To put it rightly, I think, the practice of prayer and the practice of compassion are both necessary and complementary spiritual practices. Over the last twenty years of extensive travel, going from parishes to churches, diocesan offices to social agencies, lectures to retreats, one kind of church convening to another, constantly bumping into people of faith, I find myself repeatedly impressed by the centeredness, the appealing presence, the breadth of spirit, the great-heartedness, the wholeness, indeed the joy of those whom I know to be people of committed and determined compassion and prayer. We are called to be both activists *and* mystics, missionaries of love *and* contemplatives, great lovers *and* deep thinkers. And, in all of that, the spiritual journey can happen; in all of that, we can be made whole; in all of that, the world can be made whole.

Since the Second Vatican Council, the language of spirituality has certainly enjoyed something of a flowering. A word that was never used and poorly understood by my Catholic parents is now a familiar piece of the Catholic/Christian/religious lexicon. The language of spirituality speaks to becoming, maturation, integration, personal awareness, and a felt sense of the sacred and holy. So much could and should be said and celebrated about this vivification of such an important religious concept.

With that said, I offer the following observation with some trepidation that I will sound grouchy and self-righteous. (Perhaps I am grouchy and self-righteous, but my wife, Maggie, says "not true… most of the time.") It seems to me that there is an awful lot that describes itself as Christian spirituality that is glaringly devoid of any sense of feeding the hungry, clothing the naked, or visiting those in prison. Much of Christian spirituality—indeed, much of what we call church or Christianity—seems, sadly, disengaged from the message of Jesus and the embrace of an authentic and inclusive love—what Pope Francis calls "mercy."

To describe this in one succinct experience, several years ago, Maggie and I attended a weekend sponsored by the Center for Action and Contemplation on the "Spirituality for the Second Half of Life," featuring presentations by Richard Rohr, Ronald Rolheiser, and Edwina Gately. Prior to the formal conference, there was a preconference event that highlighted the reflections of some folks who were working on human trafficking issues in Africa, which Maggie and I were grateful to attend. It was lightly attended, perhaps because it involved an extra day that people would have to take off from work. In any event, the speakers described and reflected on their work, which was nothing short of extraordinary and heroic, addressing such profound human pain and crisis. Maggie and I were in awe. At the question-and-answer period, one middle-aged man asked, in a respectful, good-natured way, why this preconference event was offered, since this was a conference on spirituality. He gracefully admitted he did not understand the connection.

M Y WORRY IS that much of what passes for spirituality and spiritual practice—prayer days, meditation, retreats, spiritual direction, contemplation, ritual, and study—is primarily informed by an exclusive attention to the self and perhaps family relationships, suggesting that much of what we call spirituality is actually some mixture of psychology and private devotion, made sacred by the use of religious imagery. My argument is not that it's worthless, but that it's woefully incomplete. I am concerned that it provides a very limited experience of what Jesus seems so passionate about, namely the "Reign of God" (the most-repeated phrase in the four Gospels).

As I understand the Reign of God, it includes the grace-driven, love-driven transformation of the self *and* the world; what's more, it recognizes that the transformation of self and world are directly connected to each other. Richard once said something to this effect: "The state of the soul is the state of the social order." The world cannot be changed by love to become just unless we are changed by love to become whole, *but* we cannot be made whole without engaging in the work of making the world whole. Personal transformation and social transformation are one piece.

Isn't it instructive that the spiritual formation of the original disciples happens with Jesus *on the road*? In effect, the disciples learn by doing. They grow into an understanding of this God of love, this God of compassion, this God who loves justice, this God who makes all things new, by participating as active observers and agents of love, compassion, justice, and newness! And, yes, necessarily, they pause with Jesus to reflect, ask questions (sometimes stupid questions), and pray. But the spiritual adventure described in the four Gospels does not happen in the sanctuary; it happens on the road, in the company of beggars, prostitutes, and lepers.

The spiritual life is perhaps best described by drawing from one of Pope Francis' favorite phrases; he insists that we're all called to be "missionary disciples," that is, people who deliberately place ourselves in the company of the world's wounds, seeking communion, healing, new possibilities, hope, and life. If this is true, then anything that describes itself as concerned with spirituality will necessarily be connected to geography! If we are to be attentive to the world's reality, with special attention to its suffering, we must position our bodies and hearts accordingly. As a matter of spiritual growth, we will eat, pray, and breathe in unexpected places.

The true spiritual quest is not that I become whole. Informed by the belief that the world is birthed by God and is precious and sacred and *one*, the true spiritual quest is that the world become whole—and we along with it. •

Failure and Perfection

By James Alison

A S A SMALL CHILD, I had two favourite picture books. One was *Ferdinand the Bull*, whom I loved to see sitting under the cork tree smelling flowers while the bullfighters raged. Of the other, I cannot remember the title, but its story and pictures have stuck with me. It was about a rotund and happy-looking friar or monk. He wanted to build a church so as to glorify God, and he set about doing just that with suitable supplies of stone and wood. It turned out that his desire to please God was much greater than his competence as a stonemason or builder, and his construction collapsed and looked for all the world like a pile of rubble.

As you can imagine, he sat around looking despondent for a while, thinking himself a total failure. But, before too long, he heard a pained meowing and, looking around, saw a cat stuck up a tree. Helping himself to some of his rubble, he hurried to build a precarious-looking pile and, although he was short and plump, he managed to bring the cat down to safety.

Other similar events occurred and, before long, an agglomeration of beasts of different sorts were sheltering under the rubble or using it for various purposes. Our friar was in clover. Surrounded by a loving congregation of a type for which he had never sought to provide, he had discovered what he had really been meant to construct all along. We were left, at the end of the book, with his rosy-cheeked beatitude as he relished the perfection of where he ended up.

The book's lesson—that perfection is not the opposite of failure, and that failure is rather its friend—was, of course, lost on me for several decades between my early childhood, when it was clear enough, and high adulthood. In the intervening years, ambition, aspiration, determination, and resolve—a firm sense of where I was going—had taken their cruel hold of me, giving me to be who I thought I was. By about the age of forty, however, I had had significant experience of failure; there was plenty of ecclesiastical-looking rubble scattered around my life, and nothing remotely like a standing church. Then I remembered my childhood picturebook with affection, wondering if perchance there might be any equivalents of cats-up-a-tree or other beasts whom I would have the pleasure of meeting amidst the patternless chaos of my rubble.

And so, of course, there have been and are.

I share all this since I hope it explains why I have a high positive regard for perfection. For those who have never seriously failed, perfection, when it is not an addiction (and therefore obviously a pathology), is so often an irritant: an enemy of the ordinary good, bringing with it a gnawing sense of insatisfaction at every endeavour and, often enough, envy at others' successes. When those who have yet to undergo failure discuss perfection philosophically it becomes, frankly, a bit of a bore, leading to definitions of what things, or experiences, *should* be, with little reference to what they are, or who the people really are who are supposed to be having them.

From the gateway, however, that is opened up to us by serious failure—for instance, of career, or marriage, or even a reputation-destroying moral lapse—perfection is indeed something rather wonderful: a dynamic sense that comes towards us from other-than-ourselves, something given that cannot be grasped and in which we can rest and delight; in short, a hint of God giving God-self away.

I think that this goes straight back to what is most basic in Christianity, which is that, out of love for us, God came among us as a failure. The image of God-self, by which God wished to let us know what God is like, was that of an apparent failure: One who was not rescued from failure, but whose very failure was shown to the apostolic witnesses to have been the true shape of what God's power and wisdom looked like. In John's Gospel, the last word Jesus says on the cross, τετέλεσται (*tetelestai*), is usually translated as "it is finished" or "it is accomplished," though it could just as well be translated "it is perfected" or, simply, as an expression of something perceived or achieved: "perfection!" The Epistle to the Hebrews picks this up when it points out that Jesus was perfected in going to his death: "he was made perfect by the things he underwent" (2:10; cf 5:8–9). The same Epistle also points out that he did this joyfully: "for the joy that was set before him, he endured the cross, despised the shame, and is seated at the right hand of God" (12:2).

But what a bizarre notion of perfection this is! In order to try to make some sense of it, I'm going to ask you to do some imagining.

Imagine that you live in a stable world, in which most people (including yourself, of course) are mostly good; some pecadillos, of course, but mostly good. From this starting point, it would seem that belief in God means that you can get a sense, from what is around you, of the goodness of God. There is a straightforward link between the things you see—the hugeness of mountains, the beauty of hummingbirds, and the power of waves, for instance—and the hugeness and beauty and power of God. Naturally, you have to multiply those created qualities many times over to come close to those of God, in whom they are perfected, but basically they are on the same pitch. Then you can also look around at others who are not good—those in need of redemption, who are genuinely not good at all: traitors, murderers, addicts, rapists, loan-sharks, price-gougers, people-traffickers. You can imagine why God, in God's goodness, wanted to knock them into shape, which he did by sending a redeemer to die for them so that they could be converted and be conformed to that good order which you respect, and could grow in ways to which you aspire.

Of course, since you are a good Catholic, or a good Christian, you make a polite nod in the direction of being in need of forgiveness

…out of love for us, God came among us as a failure.

yourself, even go to confession from time to time. But there is a difference between you and those people: there is a straight line between your life, your sense of order, and that of God, while there is only rupture between their lives and that of God.

The shocking thing about the Apostolic Witness to the perfection of Jesus' failure and what it means for us is that it explodes that picture for good. For it was the goodness, the beauty, and the order of this world, which seemed so stable, so fine, and so much like God, which was turned on its head by the realisation that all the goodness, the beauty, the power, the wisdom, and, yes, the perfection of God had shown itself to us in the misery, pain, sorrow, shame, and death of one accused of blasphemy and sedition.

What this means is that God's perfection is always, always, going to appear to us as more of a rupture than a continuation of any of our senses of perfection—and that entering into that rupture in order to experience a re-creation is not the preserve of "bad people," whom we call failures, but a necessity for all of us. For the very goodness to which we cling—our much-prized virtues and the stability that they seem to bring to our social life—is at least as much of an obstacle, if not more, to our finding ourselves on the inside of the great adventure of new creation, as anything bad we may do—the sorts of thing which might land us in shame, failure, and loss of face and reputation. And the weakness that comes with failure is the place within which the power and dynamic of the new creation most fruitfully dwells, and from which the line to perfection is most straightforwardly drawn. This is what St. Paul tells us himself in 2 Corinthians 12:9: "but [the Lord] said to me, 'My grace is sufficient for you, for my power is made perfect in weakness.'"

One of the most difficult things for any of us who try to live, and to share, the Christian story is to be faithful to two apparently contradictory pulls. On the one hand, there is the hugeness of the rupture between what might seem perfect to us and what we are astounded to discover are the sort of moments of perfection which are only available to us when we are at the end of our tether, or beyond it. And, on the other hand, there is the sense that we are loved just as we are, that we are safe, that all is well, that there is a certain contentment and satisfaction with what is. The tension is between the relaxation which we experience through the gift of faith and the sense of being stretched beyond ourselves which we experience through the gift of hope; a tension which can only be inhabited with love.

The weakness that comes with failure is the place within which the power and dynamic of the new creation most fruitfully dwells....

I'd like to look at one of the most familiar and richest of the New Testament texts concerning this tension, this perfection. This is what Our Lord teaches in Matthew 5:43–48:

> You have heard that it was said, "You shall love your neighbor and hate your enemy." But I say to you, Love your enemies and pray for those who persecute you, so you may be children of your Father in heaven; for he makes his sun rise on the evil and on the good, and sends rain on the righteous and on the unrighteous. For if you love those who love you, what reward do you have? Do not even the tax collectors do the same? And if you greet only your brothers and sisters, what more are you doing than others? Do not even the Gentiles do the same? Be perfect, therefore, as your heavenly Father is perfect.

Our Lord starts by weaning us from what seems normal: loving those close to us and hating those who threaten us. He points out that there is no link—no direct line at all—between that pattern of desire and the pattern of God's desire. In fact, our only access to God's pattern of desire is via the rupture of our learning to see our enemies as ourselves and seeking the good of those who persecute us—being towards them, completely and generously, without being over and against them in any way at all. For that is how God is: God's love for us is as love for enemies; it presupposes our hostility to God's generosity, to the fact that God is entirely removed from our sense of good and bad. The apparently banal, stable generosity we see in sunshine and rain, day and night, is in fact kept dynamically alive by a veritable storm of passionate love for those who reject and scarcely recognize it.

So we are commanded to break out of all reciprocity: not only the "tit for tat" in which we engage with our enemies, but also the *quid pro quo* in which we engage in with other insiders so as to be able to enjoy, as the failures and outcasts we will undoubtedly become in the eyes of all strong belonging systems, the huge adventure of unimaginable horizons into which we are being summoned to participate.

A sunset, a particular moment of unexpected delicacy in an operatic sextet, the tiniest turning towards love of an ungrateful child, a moment of contentment between partners in a publicly scorned relationship; these are, above all, glimpses of perfection when we have learned, in our failures, to let go of our grasp on what is good so that we can be surprised by the fierce tenderness of one who wants to overcome all our unrecognized hostility so as to crown us with glory. •

Perfection and the Harmonics of Wholeness

By David G. Benner

G IVEN OUR LIMITED experience with anything even remotely approximating perfection, the fact that humans carry within themselves a notion of the perfect is a bit of a mystery. And yet, children who have only known abuse still long for a perfect parent and lovers who have only known betrayal and disappointment still dream of the perfect partner.

As the best observers of human nature know well, very few people are as they appear. Well-constructed public masks obscure fatal flaws and parts of self that are often massively discordant with appearances. This is, of course, what makes people both interesting and incredibly frustrating.

And yet, many people find it enormously hard to tame their ideals of perfection. Life is oriented around achieving or maintaining the perfect weight or body, the perfect image, or the perfect family. The paradoxical nature of perfectionism becomes clear when we realize that all of these so-called perfections are illusions. Bodies age, images never tell the whole story, and perfect families are social fabrications. The perfection we are tempted to pursue is ultimately unattainable.

IDEALIZATION AND THE PRESERVATION OF ILLUSIONS

However, what we fail to achieve for ourselves, we easily project onto others. We do this by means of idealization. We may realize that those we idealize are not perfect, but we do see them through rose-tinted glasses that seriously distort reality.

Ultimately, idealization is always in the service of the preservation of our illusions. Sigmund Freud, who gave us the first systematic understanding of idealization, was himself caught up in a lifelong idealization of his mother. Failing to see her as she truly was meant that not only was his psychology of women fatally flawed, so were his relationships with women throughout his life. Anything that compromises our ability to see things as they truly are reduces our capacity to engage life in a vital, integral, and healthy manner.

Hero worship always involves idealization. We see this in the fact that we are enormously resistant to knowing the truth of those we idealize. But a close look at the lives of any of the most widely respected people reveals that not one of them has been or is perfect. As Nelson Mandela said to President Obama when discussing the weight of the mantle that the world had placed on him: "I am not a saint, unless you think of a saint as a sinner who keeps on trying."[1]

The visible flaw is the locus of the invisible spirit.

THE GIFT OF IMPERFECTIONS

CONSISTENCY AND PERFECTION are both seriously over-rated. In art and life, beauty is often woven around flaws. As Leonard Cohen says in the lyrics to his song *Anthem*:

Ring the bells that still can ring
Forget your perfect offering
There's a crack, a crack, in everything
That's how the light gets in.[2]

I am told that each authentic Navajo rug always has one very visible and intentional imperfection woven into it. Within Navajo spirituality, this is precisely the point where spirit moves in and out of the rug. The visible flaw is the locus of the invisible spirit. Just as in Leonard Cohen's poem, the light comes in through the crack. As Richard Rohr reminds us, perfection is not the elimination of imperfection, but the ability to recognize, forgive, and include it.[3] Only when we accept the wounds, brokenness, and imperfections can we then discover the wholeness that comes with their inclusion.

Inconsistencies, imperfections, and failures to live up to ideals are all part of what it means to be human. What seems to distinguish those who are the most deeply and wholly human is not their perfection, but their courage in accepting their imperfections. Accepting themselves as they are, they then are free to become more than they presently are. And, accepting themselves as they are, they then become able to accept others as they are.

The richness of being human lies precisely in our lack of perfection. This is the source of so much of our longing, and out of that longing emerges so much creativity, beauty, and goodness. With appropriate openness and humility, it is the cracks that let in the light. Once those cracks and flaws are embraced and accepted as part of the self, then, and only then, can the light flow out through them, into the lives of others and into the world. This is Henri Nouwen's "wounded healer"—one who mediates healing, not in spite of personal wounds, but precisely because of them.[4] It is our humanity, not our pseudo-perfection, that allows us to both receive and pass on what Christians call grace—the goodness that flows into our lives from beyond.

LIVING WHOLENESS

THE HARMONIC OF the universe is wholeness, not perfection; more specifically, it is wholeness that involves differentiation. Fusion is a union that sacrifices differentiation; wholeness retains differentiation. Without wholeness, we hear only the cacophonous noise of the various parts of our selves, clanging together. Without differentiation, we hear only the pure sound of a single tone, but not its harmonics.

If you have ever been in the Baptistery in Pisa, Italy when someone enters this incredible space and sings a single note, you will know immediately what I mean. Instead of only hearing the isolated note which is being sung, the awesome acoustics of the Baptistery allow you to hear the subtle over- and undertones of the surrounding chord that gives it the resonance of wholeness. All of life is filled with those harmonics of wholeness; sadly, we seldom hear them.

How do you know if you are on a path that leads to increasing wholeness and involves living out of wholeness? You will hear harmony, not simply the cacophony of a fragmented self. You will also sense the energy of the larger whole—an energy that goes beyond your own. You will, at least occasionally, experience the thrill of being simply a small part of a large cause, the thrill of being a tool, seized by a strong hand and put to an excellent use. You will be comforted by knowing that we are all interconnected. In a very real sense, therefore, what you do for another, you do for yourself. Love passed on to others becomes the most meaningful form of self-love and care of the earth and its inhabitants becomes care of self.

We live wholeness when we re-member our story and, through it, experience a deeper sense of being part of a greater whole. We live wholeness when we know we belong—to people, to a place, to a community and tribe, to earth, to God (however named), and to the cosmos. We live wholeness when we feel a deep sense of responsibility to live generatively by helping those younger than us—and those not yet born—to live, and to live well. We live wholeness when we know that what we already have is enough and that all we need is to be resourceful with it.

Living wholeness is participating in the dynamism of love that gathers everything together into greater unity and consciousness. It is to live with an openness of mind and heart, to encounter others, not

The richness of being human lies precisely in our lack of perfection.

as strangers, but as parts of one's self. When we enter into the heart of love in this way, we enter the field of relatedness and come to know our truest and deepest belonging and calling.

Wholeness and love are inseparable. Love leads to larger wholes and there is no true wholeness that is not built on love. In the words of Ilia Delio, "Our challenge today is to trust the power of love at the heart of life, to let ourselves be seized by love, to create and invent ways for love to evolve into a global wholeness of unity, compassion, justice, and peacemaking."[5] This is living wholeness and love.

Spare me perfection. Give me instead the wholeness that comes from embracing the full reality of who I am, just as I am. Paradoxically, it is this whole self that is most perfect. As it turns out, wholeness, not perfection, is the route to the actualization of our deepest humanity. •

This article has been adapted from David G. Benner, Human Being and Becoming *(Grand Rapids, MI: Brazos Press, 2016). Used with permission.*

Perfection

By Timothy King

I HAVE a problem with it.

There is quite possibly no concept that has been the source of more guilt and shame in my life than this one.

My problem is simple: I am not perfect.

The reality of my imperfection has the power to set off shame-inducing internal diatribes, directed at myself, that make me want to do nothing more with my life than order Chinese takeout and binge-watch bad television on Netflix.

Jesus hasn't made it any easier for me. In fact, his words in Matthew 5:48, a simple verse tucked away in the Sermon on the Mount, have sent me into more than one mental monologue of moral flagellation.

"Be perfect, therefore, as your heavenly Father is perfect." There it is. The command is clear. The law is set. Be perfect; nothing less.

The only choice left to me is whether or not I want spring rolls or crab Rangoon with my main course of guilt-fried shame.

To be conceptually aware of grace and mercy is not the same as living in their reality. I've struggled a lot more than I have admitted with going down that slippery spiral of guilt, set off every time I remember I will never attain perfection.

For a long time, this meant I tried to avoid verses like Matthew 5:48, to skirt around those shame spirals. But, in the past few years, I've started taking a different approach. Instead of running from the idea of perfection and my ensuing hang-ups, I've started to embrace the whole messy batch of feelings and pull them close. I've started to examine these incidences more closely and get a better sense of why it might be that, in the places God has declared grace and forgiveness, I seem so focused on needing to sit down in every mud puddle of shame and doubt.

A good dose of 2 Corinthians 12:9, "My grace is sufficient for you, for power is made perfect in weakness," has helped. But, instead of just skirting around a tough verse like Matthew 5:48, I've tried to dive into it and see why this command to "be perfect" troubles me so much—and, through understanding why it disturbs me, learn more about myself and the one who said it.

While tightly woven together, there have been two distinct ways of approaching this verse for me. The first has been the personal: What in my life does this idea of perfection trigger? Why does it do that? How can I change that pattern?

The second is related, but a little more cerebral. Are the words that I am hearing and internalizing actually the words Jesus wants me to hear? Another way to put it might be, when I read Matthew 5:48, am I learning more about my own personal hang-ups, struggles, and the negative aspects of my culture, or am I actually hearing the transformative message of the Gospel as Jesus intended to present it? What can I learn about the language, the context, and the history of this passage that might allow me to be in a more productive conversation with it?

I'll start with understanding; to understand this verse, there are some important words to delve into, context to understand, and framework to explore for the entire Sermon on the Mount.

SERMON ON THE MOUNT

IF THE SERMON on the Mount (Matthew 5–7) was to be awarded a superlative by its peers, it might very well come away with Most Likely to Be Watered Down by Nervous Preachers. I've run into

more than a few Christians who insist on the importance of believ-
ing in a literal seven-day creation period that happened six thousand
years ago and will perform mental feats of wonder in order to explain
exactly how Noah got all those critters onto his boat, but, when it
comes to "blessed are those who mourn" or "turn the other cheek," it
becomes quite clear that they believe Jesus didn't want us to take him
too seriously.

There are lots of ways to rationalize and contextualize the
Sermon on the Mount that tone down its bite. It's also technically
possible to remove the kick from a good cask-strength bourbon
whiskey and drink alcohol-free, brown corn-water instead, but I'm
really not sure what the point would be.

The point of digging more into the context of Matthew 5:48 is
not to try and search out as many reasons as I can to lower the bar so
that I no longer feel uncomfortable, but to try and learn as much as
I can so that, when I do feel uncomfortable, it's because I'm learning
and growing.

For this, I do what I normally do when I am perplexed by a
particular passage of Scripture. I find out what my old college professor,
Scot McKnight, has to say about it. In *Sermon on the Mount*, McKnight
identifies part of the problem with interpreting this verse in that
the focus falls solely on how to read the word "perfect." Instead, he
observes, "Perhaps the most neglected feature in probing the meaning
of 'perfect' is the word 'as'...."[1]

Often, this problem is approached by taking a look at the Greek
word τέλειος (*teleios*), used in the text, which is often defined as
"completion," "perfect," "mature," "adult," or "full development." But
Jesus probably wasn't speaking Greek, so another approach is to look
at the Hebrew or Aramaic and focus on the words שָׁלֵם (*shalem*) or
תָּמִים (*tamim*), which could be translated as "unblemished" or "whole."

McKnight runs through these possibilities and notes that,
because of the context of the phrase and comparing it to other uses of
the word, many conclude, "The notion, then, is not the rigor of sinless-
ness but the rigor of utter devotion."[2]

McKnight thinks there is more to unearth. This is why he also
focuses on the word "as." Jesus is not just giving a general admoni-
tion to his followers to be rigorously devoted to God, but is giving
particular moral weight to something specific within the character
of the Father.

A few verses earlier, this section starts off with the familiar Sermon on the Mount refrain, "You have heard that it was said." In this section, Jesus tells his followers, "You shall love your neighbor and hate your enemy. But I say to you, Love your enemies and pray for those who persecute you" (5:43–44).

Jesus is not demanding that his followers throw on some light switch in their soul that will lead them to forever-sinless lives. Rather, he is calling on a persecuted people, living under Roman occupation, with the everyday threat to life, family, and homes, to be so utterly devoted to radically redefining what it means to "love your neighbor" that it will encompass even loving your enemies and praying for your persecutors.

It would not be long before Jesus showed this utter devotion to his Father by praying on the cross for his judge, jury, and executioners to be forgiven.

APPLICATION

I'VE CONVERTED TO Christianity—a lot. Growing up, I took almost every chance I was offered to raise my hand, walk down the aisle, fill out a form, or just say a small, quiet prayer in my heart.

My pattern was simple. I'd make a commitment to Christ, feel great excitement and moral purpose for one to two weeks, fall back into the life of adolescent sin, determine that my prayer for salvation hadn't "worked," then wait until the next opportunity and hope, next time, it would stick.

Luckily, I had teachers and pastors in my life who tried to disabuse me of these patterns and ways of thinking. But, even as I could acknowledge conceptually that this wasn't how grace worked, it didn't necessarily change my mode of being.

I viewed my faith as a race. My conversion was the starting gun that set me off down the road. Those first stretches I would approach with zeal and energy. But, in no time, my breath would run short, I'd have a cramp in my stomach, and my legs would start to feel like lead. I'd tell myself, "I must have done something wrong at the start; I need to go back and begin again." One of these times, I figured, I'd start so well that I'd get straight through to the finish line without ever slowing down.

...shame can have no place in us as we embrace the goodness with which God has created us.

I figured there wasn't much point in moving forward until I knew how to do it right, until I could "be perfect" as I had been commanded to be. At best, I felt like I was running around half a circle and then stumbling back to finish the loop. At worst, I felt like I was sliding down endless spirals of shame at never seeming to get it right.

The idea of the Christian life as a race to be run comes from Paul (e.g., Hebrews 12:1). Athletic analogies abound throughout the Church tradition, and they are helpful. But, if your vision is of a race that you lose and need to quit if you ever grow tired or trip up, even once, then you are in for a life lived in that spiral of shame.

But what if, at the same time you are running the race, you are also training for it? One mile a day for the first week isn't a week of failure. Rather, it's the only way you could ever hope to run two miles a day the second week.

Grace is the gift we get to try again, every day, and it transforms the downward spiral of shame to a "widening circle" of mercy. For me, it's been helpful to break away from the athletic analogies altogether. In Rilke's book of poetry, *The Divine Hours,* he gives a beautiful description of this process:

> I live my life in widening circles
> that reach out across the world.
> I may not complete this last one
> but I will give myself to it.
>
> I circle around God, around the primordial tower.
> I've been circling for thousands of years
> and I still don't know: am I a falcon,
> a storm, or a great song?[3]

There are two important affirmations in this poem. First, we can live our life in widening circles. We are not stuck in a closed loop with no hope of improvement or movement. We can give ourselves to this outer circle even while understanding that we have not attained it. That utter devotion to what we haven't yet achieved becomes a source of strength that keeps us moving upward instead of a badge of shame that pushes us down.

The second affirmation is that, if you ever feel like you are just going in circles, you aren't alone. We are often trained to think of life as being lived in a linear fashion but, many times, we'll experience life in a cyclical pattern, where we keep returning to old lessons and habits. This is not an excuse for us not to grow, but is a reminder not to feel discouraged at needing to learn the same lessons more than once; often, over and over!

Jesus gives us that vision: the widening circle that we might never complete, to which we give ourselves anyway. McKnight describes it this way:

> There is only one approach to living the words of this [Matthew 5:48] text. It begins when we confess who is our enemy and it ends when we learn to love them as our neighbor. Until we name our enemies we can't live these words of Jesus. Until we invite them into our home or treat them as our neighbor, or love them as we love ourselves, we do not live these words. Until we regard them and dwell with them and embrace them as God regards, dwells with, and embraces them, we cannot live these words of Jesus.[4]

When confronted with a possible spiral of shame, I now turn to Matthew 5:48 instead of running from it. This passage is not an esoteric command that we must shoulder as a burden just because it is in Scripture. Rather, when it is well-understood, it provides deep words of wisdom for living a complete and full life. These are words that help us to flourish in valuable ways.

First, the verse presents us with a challenge. While the crowds listening to this sermon would have had the Romans on their minds when it came to enemies, I believe it also applies when we make an enemy out of ourselves.

Shame comes from our rejection of the deep truth that God created us good. The great deception that controls our lives when we live in shame is that our True Self is our greatest enemy. If we live into the deepest truth of Matthew 5:48, shame can have no place in us as we embrace the goodness with which God has created us.

Second, instead of looking down in shame because of our imperfections, it gives us a place to look toward in hope. To know our heavenly Father is perfect, in the way Jesus describes, is to know that we are not enemies of God, but beings to whom God extends the greatest love, boundless grace, and resounding mercy.

That is the road to being perfect as our Heavenly Father is perfect. Matthew 5:48 is more disturbing and life-giving to me than ever before and, though I might never fully reach that place, I give myself to it. •

The Trap of Perfectionism:

Two Needed Vulnerabilities

By Richard Rohr

I HAVE NEVER PARTICULARLY liked the fact that I am an Enneagram Type One. The passion for the One is a self-created perfectionism, which makes us always dissatisfied and disappointed in just about everything, starting with ourselves. Our inner critic is quite well-trained and practiced, and it takes years of inner work to recognize how completely this critical worldview impairs our perception and keeps us from our natural compassion. Yet it is also our greatest gift, if the negative edges are rubbed off and we can see things in a much more nuanced, positive, and less-demanding way.

The only way through for me, the only freedom I find, is in a very real and very pricey vulnerability, instead of this false search for the perfect. In *Daring Greatly*, Brené Brown, a contemporary master teacher in the area of vulnerability and shame, writes that "Vulnerability is not knowing victory or defeat, it's understanding the necessity of both; it's engaging. It's being all in."[1] She describes "all in" as to "dare to show up and let ourselves be seen."[2] For me, to be "all in" is to live on a perpetual cusp, somewhere between total victory and total defeat. I experience this as a continuous vulnerability, but as two very different shapes and kinds of vulnerability, both appearing to me as the only way out of the trap. (The Latin root meaning of vulnerability is "a capacity to carry a wound"; *vulnera* = wound.)

I suspect there is a bit of perfectionism—in one area or another—in almost all people I know, even if they are addicted to being perfectly sloppy or proudly imperfect! It shows itself in those many compulsive, repetitive, and self-defeating patterns in which we all engage. We are each sure that our chosen and habitual behavior is the *effective and right* way to do the task at hand, which is why we can persist in so much self-defeating behavior for much of our lives, while still expecting things to get better. Perfection is invariably our own self-created notion, manufactured largely in our own thinking mind or by our era or culture; thus it is both delusional and, finally, self-defeating—as well as a major enemy and obstacle to loving what is right in front of us.

Only God can lay claim to perfection. Yet we keep plowing ahead, demanding a desired and expected response from ourselves and from the world, even when we seldom get it. We then use this disappointing information to notice everyone else's imperfection! Such a false crusade only gets more compulsive and demanding, the older we get.

For some strange reason, we seldom bother to call our own definition of perfection into question, even though it keeps us in endless envy, comparison, and competition, along with far too much shame and inadequacy. Few are prepared to help us see the foundational and false source for all this perfectionistic energy. It takes largely unknown myths like Sisyphus to reveal what is, in fact, hidden in plain sight. We are eternally pushing a rock up our own carefully selected hill and, even though it forever rolls back down on us, we keep trying the torturous ascent one more time. It is the Greek description of hell. It is a road to nowhere, except unhappiness for all concerned.

To overcome our futile obsession with perfection, we have to hold both victory and defeat together in the same breath and same moment and, as Brené Brown says, "understand the necessity of both."

Yes, my deepest knowledge is a knowledge and experience of profound goodness at the heart of everything....

Vulnerability refuses to define itself merely as the wounding that comes from defeat. Believe it or not, there is wounding—especially in our secular and sophisticated society—that comes from admitting and accepting our deepest inner victory, which is the inherent dignity held by our very soul. It knows and holds our identity as a daughter and son of God. Such dignity does not come and go, it stands and holds and gives. This now feels very naïve and foolish, a mere whistling in the dark, a simpleton's hope. I will try to explain, and hope that it makes sense to you.

The real victory for me was when I was able to recognize my profound inner experience of *goodness as the core and foundation of all reality.* It amounts to the very discovery of my soul! This belief grounds all my hope and desire, and my very willingness to enjoy life. It almost brings me to tears when I think about it. It is my deepest "little boy," looking out at life with utter *innocence* (of which the Latin root means "unwoundedness"). To be vulnerable about this is to lose my innocence and to be wounded at the core. *Yes, my deepest knowledge is a knowledge and experience of profound goodness at the heart of everything—which is always begging to be known, even through me.*

It is, in fact, as embarrassing and mostly impossible for me to accept and love this naïve and simple little boy as it is to painfully accept the defensive games by which I protect him. My little boy is my deepest soul, my unwounded innocence, my insistence on the one, the true, and the beautiful in all things, which God has allowed me to see. He is even harder to allow and accept than the bulletproof and false persona that I present to protect him. They are two different kinds of vulnerability, but they are both a necessary wounding to break through to a Larger Beauty that is bigger than my tiny definition of perfection. God's perfection is able to include imperfection;

what else could divine perfection be? The road to get to divine perfection is a long one. For me, it is the very shape and goal of any mature spirituality, which somehow moves from a self-created *order*, to tragic *disorder*, and on to a *reorder* that is not of our making.

But back to my attempt at describing the conflict: Any personal or public presentation of my core innocence feels to me like I am exaggerating, lying, idealizing myself, being presumptuous, or making myself into a little saint that no one would believe, like, or trust. I fear that no one would take me seriously and that I, myself, am just pretending. My little boy is lost in idealism, and we Americans all need and admire a kind of pragmatic realism that pervades our Yankee, can-do culture. My way out has always been to write about spirituality or speak about this inner goodness in a very objective and theological way. I became a preacher and a teacher, where I could always have the answer, but not a self-revealing novelist or dramatist. This very article is probably as close as I will ever come to any kind of autobiography.

My deepest truth is like that fragile little boy within me, begging for protection through an endless litany of words, sermons, books, and webcasts. He is largely hidden from my hour-by-hour perception. Without doubt, my little soul-child is my only place of total victory and rest, and yet I hold him so tenderly, and with constant fear and doubt. Am I kidding myself? Is this all merely wishful thinking? I quite literally *lose my soul* whenever I become negative, cynical, or judgmental, most especially about myself. For each of us, our soul is so easily lost, except when we can be vulnerable and poor—and surrender to both our very best and our sometimes-worst. These are two equal vulnerabilities for me. "Sinners" are those who surrender to their very worst; "saints" are those who surrender to their very best. I am both.

When I see violence, mean-spiritedness, cruelty, gratuitous destruction, crass ambition, obvious deceit, or mistreatment of animals, I almost cannot bear it. I want to look away, and I am sure this feels like *naïveté* to most people. I try to pretend it did not happen; I turn off the TV or leave the movie early. "This cannot be true! I will not let it be true! It is an utter defacing of what I know to be, in fact, the case. Badness must not be allowed to win!" And then I jump like a white knight on my white charger to rearrange reality into the way it is supposed to be.

I hate cynicism in myself and others almost more than anything else, precisely because I have to resist it every day of my life. If I would finally fall into the pit of cynicism, which is a foundational mistrust of foundational goodness, there would be no way out for me. If reality is all not-good at the core, I have no ground, no direction, and no hope. So I keep wearing my armor, always in defense of the good, the true, and the beautiful. Yet, with supreme irony, it is only when I take off that armor that the healing waves of goodness and universal empathy can flow over and through me.

In defense of this precious and all-important goodness at the heart of everything, I present a bulletproof exterior—Richard: whole, entire, and believable—to the world. Do you see how my love of foundational goodness makes me flirt with a constant "badness"? Does that make sense at all? My worst badness comes from doubting and over-defending my objective goodness. Is this perhaps one way

My little boy is my deepest soul, my unwounded innocence, my insistence on the one, the true, and the beautiful in all things....

of stating the core human conflict? Is this especially the fate of all zealots and true believers? Is it somehow the fate of everybody?

Only a vulnerable admission, on *both* sides of the question—my goodness or my badness—gives me a way out and a way through. They are equally painful and humbling recognitions, but in very different ways. I must resist hating either of them. *Both are wounds, but they are also sacred wounds.* We must be fully forgiving and engaged with both of these wounding truths—we have to be "all in," and this takes so much time, patience, and complete honesty with ourselves.

Only some hidden grace allows me to walk on this tightrope, but the tightrope is always there to traverse if I allow it.

As a man, a priest, a self-contained celibate, a public figure, and a spiritual teacher, I have a thousand good reasons and excuses to present a perfect persona to the outer world. I really do not have to be vulnerable *until it is demanded of me!* And, because I am usually the leader or central person in most settings, I am also rather accustomed to being in control and "important." Some regular experiences of vulnerability are *the only way* out of this tender trap.

God alone helps me to love reality as it is, but it is still and always, somehow, a defeat! It is always a kind of crucifixion and surrender of *the idea of goodness for which I long*—instead of the actual goodness that is given. I have learned that I, Richard, cannot protect some notion of perfection, nor do I need to promote my notion of perfection; only God defines and knows what perfection is. Then I note that God's strategic plan seems to be about mercy and forgiveness—of almost everything.

So my demand for perfection is surely my worst fault and my greatest gift. As Paul says, "Death is at work in me, but life in you" (see 2 Corinthians 4:12). I believe this is true for every one of us! If we face our core goodness, it is actually a kind of absolute and embarrassing surrender; and if we face our defensive games, this is an equally embarrassing surrender—two necessary vulnerabilities. Only then does a much larger perfection fall through the cracks of my own life, and I am able to trust that it will always be there, even without my efforts to personify it or, in any way, create it. It seems to be from an Inexhaustible Source. •

Perfection as an Experience of Presence and Grace

By Russ Hudson

O NE OF THE greatest challenges on the spiritual journey is recognizing the difference between the various authentic qualities of the soul—the qualities of Divine Grace that make our spiritual development possible—and the various ways our ego self tries to understand and be, or *have*, these qualities. The ego has its uses and, when it takes its proper place, is a necessary part of our development. But when it comes to the subtler and more profound truths of the spirit—that to which faith calls us—the ego is bound to get us into trouble because it cannot really understand them.

This distinction becomes more important as we seek to deepen our spiritual life and to really follow the teachings of the great saints and mystics. It certainly comes into play if we are seeking to authentically understand and follow the fundamental teachings of Jesus. As our spirituality matures, we come to understand that we may spend our entire lives discovering new levels of meaning in one of the parables or the teachings of the Sermon on the Mount, for example. When encountering any real spiritual teaching, our ego tends to interpret the teaching in ways congruent with its limited understanding. More problematically, the more fixated and fear-based ego seeks to "rework" the truth found there into something more congruent with its own agenda.

This is not a new issue, obviously, but it is a mark of spiritual maturity when we can discern the difference between the more automatic interpretations we have of sacred texts and teachings and the effect of really living with them and exploring them in light of our experience. We do not so quickly assume that we know what a particular spiritual concept or teaching means and, even if we have had previous insights into a teaching, we remain curious and open to new revelations and insights. We learn to *contemplate* spiritual teachings rather than bind ourselves to a fixed view about them.

The same is true in our relationship with our own place of inner knowing—which is distinct from our opinions and historic views. We learn to become more sensitive and receptive, and to pay attention to the deepest places in our hearts, listening to the great silence within us—the place from which God speaks. It is from here that we begin to feel into the real meanings of the terms and teachings we have encountered. And it is also from here that we can see the various ego impulses in us that tend to "lead us into temptation." As these distinctions become more practiced and natural for us, we also recognize that what can correct our "wayward" impulses is not gritting our teeth and forcing some notion of goodness upon ourselves and others.

The whole concept of "perfection" makes this matter abundantly clear. Most of us, upon hearing this word, will instantly seize upon various concepts, acquired during the course of our lives, which we associate with being perfect. We may well have notions of moral perfection, artistic perfection, job perfection, relationship perfection, and spiritual perfection. If we really look at this carefully, we will likely notice that, in each case, we have a notion from our past about how these things are *supposed to be*. Generally speaking, when we hold these views of a perfect anything, we are largely *not* aware of any good that is happening now. Our ideas of perfection are likely of something higher, perhaps very rare and exceptional, even

...sacredness seems to be inherently part of every moment when we remember to be awake, to contemplate, and to be open and receptive to the presence of God.

otherworldly, yet we do not associate perfection with a quality of the moment we are actually experiencing. In short, our ideas about perfection tend to blind us to most of what is amazing and sacred in the present moment.

Yet, when we are quieter inside, when we relax and open to the living presence of this moment, we will usually, to our great surprise and delight, feel something absolutely right about the present moment. Yet this "rightness" is not the result of any particular cause. There is no specific element that is creating it, nor is there any specific element that is ruining it. We may also experience it as *the sense of the sacred,* and it is good to notice that this sacredness seems to be inherently part of every moment when we remember to be awake, to contemplate, and to be open and receptive to the presence of God. Then we are at a much better vantage point to understand something of that to which the word "perfection" might be pointing.

S o w h a t i s perfection as an experience of presence and grace? We may initially recognize this as a quality of *goodness* that seems to permeate everything we are experiencing. We sense there is indeed something good about the world, and about our existence, that is independent of any of our ideas of goodness. We might not be inclined to call it perfection just yet, but we notice that this quality of goodness feels positive and benevolent. As we relax more deeply into this sensibility, we may also recognize it as a sense of lucid intelligence and implicit order that seems to pervade our experience. Things make more sense. We feel more aligned with reality and more naturally part of things. This sense cannot be rationalized, and it is not easily explained. Yet, when we surrender more deeply to the present moment, we cannot help but notice it. It reminds us that there is indeed something good and noble moving through us and seeking expression. It becomes much easier to believe that we are indeed beloved of God. In fact, everything we behold seems blessed and dignified in this fresh and alert sense of what we are experiencing as the world.

One could argue that this would only be true when things are going well, when fortune is smiling on us. But I would invite us to consider that, often, when things are going our way, we are *less* likely to notice the goodness of life and to take credit for whatever good is happening. Or, more typically, we may just take our good fortunes for granted. By contrast, it is often when we are having our most difficult times, when we are facing misfortune or loss, when we are at the bed-side of a dying loved one, that we are more likely to see these qualities of goodness, of blessing, of the nobility of this life and of the soul's journey. In such moments, we are much less likely to take *anything* for granted. We may recognize that the very losses we are experiencing are causing us to shed our usual fantasies and distractions, and we feel much closer to something true and fundamental about life—although perhaps harder to express in words.

Yet, when things are going well by any normal standards, we can feel frustrated and quite far from any sense of goodness or purity or nobility. What we tend to forget, again and again, is that this sense of agitation is not being caused by a particular person or situation. My reaction to them is *my* reaction and others may have quite different reactions. We can become excessively harsh with ourselves as a way of trying to force ourselves to more closely correspond to the idealized standards in our minds and consequently create great suffering for ourselves and others. As we lose presence, we lose the direct experience of the Divine, and our hearts suffer and react. We assume something has gone horribly wrong. How can the world be like this? How did God let this happen? We feel that the "higher-ups" surely have been making some big mistakes, and our poor ego feels responsible for rectifying them. How does this happen?

As our ego patterns take form in the inevitable challenges and disappointments of our early childhood development, we increasingly lose the capacity to be present and, with that, the sense of the goodness in us and around us. In the process, we become more agitated and frustrated. The ideal situation does *not* seem to be occurring, and we want "the good stuff back." Indeed, our entire underlying feeling and sense of ourselves becomes flavored with this deeply unsettled, agitated, aggravated state. In the Enneagram work, this is called the passion of Angry Resentment and it is associated with point One.[1]

We also begin to divide our experience into good and bad, right and wrong, sacred and profane. In other words, we fall under the spell of the dualistic mind and, as we do so, we want to rally around and protect what we think is good and true while separating ourselves from what we have decided is lower and bad. Now, the dualistic mind has its place; we need both inner and outer discrimination in our lives. But when this discriminating mind gets detached from the deeper ground of non-dual consciousness—the part of us that directly knows and experiences the sacred—all manner of confusion and suffering ensues. Cut off from its natural ground, the discriminating mind stops being a tool of understanding and becomes more of a defense of what we see as the good in us and against what we perceive as the bad and imperfect in us. Unfortunately, this detached mental process is in no position to actually recognize where goodness lies, much less how to act in accordance with it. It is born from fear, not faith, and yet it can utterly come to dominate our spiritual lives. It erects an ideal, created from memories of experiences of goodness which may have been true at the time, but that now actually prevent us from being open to the goodness in *this* moment. This ideal is fiercely held and defended by ego consciousness and sets itself against reality, which is constantly measured and found wanting.

O NCE THIS IDEAL is established in our minds, we tend to fall into a pattern of judging ourselves, others, and the world. We feel the need to condemn anything that does not correspond to our notions of goodness and perfection. The Scriptures warn us in many places about the problematic nature of judging (see Romans 2:1 and 14:13, Matthew 7:1, Deuteronomy 32:35, and Proverbs 21:2, to name a few). Over and over, the scriptures warn us to let God handle the settling of scores and not to use our views about righteousness to condemn others. Paul seems to strike this point many times in the Epistles, and especially in Romans, even as he was attempting to help the early church establish the key elements it

...there is indeed something good and noble moving through us and seeking expression.

needed to function in the world. John goes so far as to remind us that Jesus too was not here to judge us (John 3:17).

The problem is that *the very part of our mind that is so valiantly trying to solve this problem is not in touch with the deeper aspects of reality that can actually do so.* This part of our psyche, often strongly related to the Freudian concept of the superego, creates a full-time mission to get things right, but does not really have the means to recognize when things actually *are* right, so to speak. It is a mind born out of the very frustration it is seeking to resolve. Usually, this structure is seeking to restore an idealized version of reality based on a vague sense-memory of when things were right. This ideal is in fact where we get the egoic notion of perfection—that way of being, living, and interacting that will be the end of the agitation and will signal that all is again right in our world. However, based as it is in a memory, the very idealized notion that we hold distracts us, over and over, from the very receptive consciousness through which we might again recognize the actual sense of goodness that is already here as an inherent element of Presence.

This mechanism in our consciousness really does not know what grace is, and is terrified to stop its activity lest we fall into chaos and evil. Yet it is often the instigator of much of the abuses we perpetrate, on ourselves and others. We endlessly abuse ourselves trying to live up to ideas of ourselves that actually alienate us from the deep and sensitive ground of our soul, the place where Divine Grace can actually meet us and work with us. We slowly learn that, as we trust the moment, as we listen, as we become receptive to the inherent goodness in reality—however it may be manifesting in this moment—this very goodness begins to shift us, to bring about a remembering in our deepest hearts and minds of the fact that we *are* beloved, noble, and lifted up by grace. There is goodness and sacredness here *right now* and, with this recognition, we are guided toward more beautifully attuned and intelligent responses to the situations in which we find ourselves.

Without this understanding, we are condemned to continually and endlessly "beat ourselves up" in an internal holy war against ourselves—the idealized idea being used as ammunition against all the ways we see ourselves as falling short of the ideal. Even though the ego here is heroically seeking to restore a sense of heaven on earth, it is hard to imagine a quicker route to hell than the self-abuse that almost inevitably arises from this pattern of judgement and self-correction. We may succumb to the passion of point One on the Enneagram—angry resentment—whether or not we are centrally identified with this point for our personality.

Again, from the ego's limited perspective, we do not see all of this. Most of what we have been discussing remains unconscious. From our point of view, we are merely trying to get things right, to come as close to perfection as we can.

For example, as I sit down to write this essay, I want it to be as "perfect" as possible. This does not feel wrong or strange—I want the best I can do for my readers, and I want to add to the fine quality of articles that will no doubt appear in this journal. I feel responsible to do a good job, the best of which I am capable. Now, of course, I have no idea what this will look like, but I do know that, if the writing is not of a quality I find acceptable, I am going to need to keep working on it, refining it, and polishing it, until I feel it is "right." I know that it will feel right at some point, but I have no way to know how and when that will happen. If I am not particularly present, and let these types of thoughts run away with me, I will have difficulty even starting this project, because the expectations cooked up by my mind will be huge and difficult to live up to. Indeed, that has happened a few times as I have prepared myself to begin writing!

But a deeper part of me knows that such perfection as may appear here is going to come from "a different place" in my psyche. I know from experience that, when I relax and trust the process of writing, also knowing that I have spent many years learning the craft of writing so I can be ready for such moments as this, words come forth that are more helpful and relevant than any of the clever plans I had been busily concocting in my head. Now, this can be tricky too, because, if I get too many ideas in my head about this, I may also wait for a perfect moment of inspiration that generally does not come in the ways I might imagine. I need to sit down at the computer, I need to relax, and I need to give over my awareness, mind, heart, and body, to what I am wishing to communicate. And, most of all, I need to be receptive. I need a quality of consciousness that is more like listening than it is like speaking. Then, by the Grace of God—as people used to say, at just the right moment, the words start flowing onto the page.

Now, many of us may not be writers or so explicitly in a creative field, but the principle applies to pretty much everything, from doing yard work, to praying or meditating, or to having an important conversation with my child. There is a way of entering into things that allows the finest and most attuned impulses in us to come forth. And much of this is accomplished, not by continually upping the expectations and pressure we place on ourselves, but by a kind of surrender and trust to the living moment—the moment in which I *experientially* encounter what feels like a Divine Intelligence, already here and knowing just how to respond.

The great miracle in all of this is that, in a single breath, in a single moment of interrupting the relentless drive of my ego to get things right, there can be a moment of quiet mercy in which I begin, however dimly, to notice that the goodness I am seeking is already here. The perfection is not something I can achieve, but, in this moment of openness and surrender, my words and actions become more informed by the implicit intelligence and order of reality, or, as it is sometimes called, the Divine Will. The sense of the sacred returns to my awareness. When this happens, there is generally little to no self-consciousness about it; no need to get credit or to evaluate myself in any way. Rather, there is a peaceful confidence and a genuine humility. I am feeling joy that, in whatever small ways, in that moment, I am remembering the goodness and perfection of Spirit and, in that remembering, I am helping to bring something truly good into this world. •

The Unbearable Suchness of Holy Perfection

Be intent upon the perfection of the present day.
—William Law

By Gayle Scott

T HE ENCHANTING FILM *Chocolat*, a delicious comic fable nominated for a 2001 Best-Picture Oscar, imaginatively illustrates both the heroic impulse and the foolish delusion of a well-intentioned character in tragic pursuit of perfection. Alfred Molina stars as the Comte de Reynaud, the imperious mayor of a quiet country village in the South of France in 1959. A pious and principled man of faith, the Comte is dedicated to protecting and maintaining the moral virtue of his little village.

In the ancient psycho-spiritual system known as the Enneagram of Personality, the Comte de Reynaud is a classic Type One character, variously known as the Reformer, the Crusader, the Moralist, and the Perfectionist.

Healthy Type One individuals are extraordinarily principled and purposeful. They are valiant truth-bearers who are naturally honest and just. As instinctive people of action, Ones are drawn to educate and advocate, to teach and preach, to investigate and legislate on behalf of their cherished convictions and ideals.

The season of Holy Lent is upon the village. As always, the devout mayor has dutifully forsaken the pleasure of all things sweet—refusing even a drop of honey for his morning tea or a spoonful of jam with his crust of bread. "My fast has been very strict this year, but how can I make demands of the townspeople if I don't demand more from myself?"

Conscientious Ones lead by example and dutifully embrace hardship and sacrifice in the name of a just or holy cause. They experience themselves as good, moral people, earnest and hardworking, determined to lead virtuous lives.

As the church bells toll on a Sunday morning, an unexpected stranger arrives in the village. Vianne Rocher, a charming, free-spirited gypsy, played by the luminous Juliette Binoche, has recently leased the vacant patisserie in the town square. The mayor is shocked to learn that Vianne is converting the old bakery into a chocolate shop—in full view of the church and during the Holy Season of Lent. "I could imagine better timing," says the disapproving mayor.

When the doors of the *Chocolaterie Maya* open for business in the town square, the curiosity of the residents (along with their neglected appetites) is intensely aroused. One by one, the villagers venture into the charming *chocolaterie*, only to succumb to the mouthwatering magic of Vianne's chocolate truffles, hot cocoa, and cakes. Seeing his wayward flock frequenting Vianne's unholy shop of horrors, the mayor becomes more and more angry and distraught.

Soon the parishioners are showing up at Pére Henrî's confessional with stories of lapsed will and broken fasts, describing their sinful indulgences to the hapless young priest in mouthwatering detail.

Each Sunday, Pére Henrî is obliged to deliver a sermon, largely composed by the mayor, charging the parishioners to "resurrect their moral awareness" and resist temptation. Despite the gravity of these warnings, the sermons are frequently accompanied by the furtive crackling sounds of *Chocolaterie Maya* candy wrappers emanating from the pews.

Scrupulously self-controlled Ones often repress their instinctual impulses and inhibit their natural human desires as they struggle to live up to their Inner Critic's increasingly ruthless ideals of moral perfection.

ALTHOUGH THE MAYOR remains resolute in his Lenten vow of abstinence, his failure to inspire similar resolve in his wayward flock eventually takes its toll. Late one night, driven by despair, the mayor breaks into the *Chocolaterie Maya*. Wielding a long dagger, he climbs into the elaborate window display, overflowing with platters of sweet, dark fudge and creamy truffles. Crawling on hands and knees, surrounded by luscious layer cakes and ornately carved chocolate creations, the frantic mayor raises his dagger and starts hacking the chocolate to pieces.

In the frenzy, a glob of gooey dark chocolate splatters across his lips. He tastes sweet temptation. Succumbing to what Freud knowingly coined "the return of the repressed," the Comte loses all self-control and gorges uncontrollably on the forbidden fruit. When his momentary madness subsides, he collapses in shame and loses consciousness in the window box.

The next morning, the Comte is discovered face-down in the ruined display, disheveled and smeared with chocolate from head to toe. He opens his eyes to see his nemesis, Vianne, whose storefront he has clearly ravaged, offering him a glass of bubbly tonic water. "Here, drink this—it will refresh you." The mayor takes the water, takes in his situation, and is utterly mortified.

After all his mighty efforts to be so very good and virtuous—to be *perfect* in his observance of the Lenten fast—and now, to have failed so miserably and fallen so visibly! The shattered mayor can summon no words. He knows, beyond a doubt, that he is facing damnation for his malicious and scandalous act. But as he looks up at Vianne, he sees only compassion and forgiveness in her eyes.

In the liberating light of her benevolent affirmation, his guilt, resentment, and rage effortlessly dissolve. His hard-won righteousness comes undone. Beheld and mirrored in Vianne's merciful gaze, the Comte de Reynaud suddenly sees, feels, and tastes the sacred substance of his own uniquely flawed humanity—and it is good. "I am so sorry," he tells her. Vianne nods and, with a conspiratorial smile, she says, "I won't tell a soul."

> When awake and present, Ones possess and administer a truly discriminating wisdom. Natural reformers and crusaders, they are often in the vanguard of vital and lasting social, environmental, spiritual, and political progress and change.

Every society, and the world at large, has benefitted from the wisdom and will of the healthy Type One Reformer/Perfectionist. Some well-known historical exemplars include the Chinese teacher and philosopher Confucius, the Greek writer and philosopher Plato, St. Paul the Apostle, St. Joan of Arc, Sir Thomas More, Father Damien (St. Damien of Moloka'i), Mahatma Gandhi, Nelson Mandela, and Pope John Paul II.

Type One personalities are strongly attracted to the idea of the Sacred. As with many of the above Reformers, the playing field—or battleground—of the One's quest for perfection often centers on their spiritual life and aspirations. Having come into this life as a Type One personality, I acknowledge that I too am a card-carrying, dues-paying member of the International Order of Perfectionists. While I don't aspire to historical significance or sainthood, I am a specialist by temperament in the pursuit and appraisal of everyday perfection.

The Holy Idea is not a concept — it is the total impact of everything that is here, right now.

The Type One soul, while abiding in Original Blessing, enjoyed a direct experience of The Sacred: the ultimate expression of Holy Perfection. In the Garden, nothing needed to be fixed or improved. Her soul was relaxed, content, and serene. During the course of early childhood ego development, each soul undergoes a traumatic process that feels like a disconnection from Source: a loss of direct contact with God. The particular suffering of the One is a chronic feeling of sinfulness. Embattled Ones wrestle with and endure what feels like an inherent badness or wrongness in themselves and in the world. A One may spend her life trying to atone for this sinfulness in order to earn her way back to the Garden.

THE RURAL TEMPLE town of Tiruvannamalai, or Tiru, in the southern province of Tamil Nadu, India, is known for attracting multitudes of spiritual seekers, pilgrims, meditators, and mystics from all backgrounds and traditions. They come seeking solitude and seclusion, extended spiritual retreat in local ashrams, or to learn and practice traditional forms of Ayurvedic medicine, contemplation, yoga, and meditation.

I had come to Mother India as a continuation of my lifelong quest to see and experience, in its many forms, the sacred unknown. Along with a passion for immersive adventures in foreign lands, I had an enduring interest in personally sampling and savoring the profound power and mystery of religious ceremonies and rituals practiced by communal societies, tribes, and cultures around the world.

Every full moon, tens of thousands of pilgrims, travelling by airplane, train, bus, motorcycle, moped, taxi, auto rickshaw, and foot, converge on Tiruvannamalai from all over India and beyond. They come to walk barefoot and clockwise the fourteen-kilometer trail that circles the holy mountain Arunachala, the home and physical embodiment of Lord Shiva, the all-pervading, uncaused, and timeless Supreme Deity. The green mountain is the sacred centerpiece of the town and is where the Indian sage and philosopher Bhagavan Sri Ramana Maharshi lived in caves, became enlightened, and founded his ashram, which serves as the spiritual center of this rural enclave on the outskirts of the city.

I hoped that a winter immersion in rural Indian Hindu culture would authenticate and deepen my thirty-year on-again-off-again meditation practice. I also had a desire to study, near its source, the enigmatic Bhagavad Gita, the seven-hundred-verse Hindu Song of the Lord composed in the fourth millennium BC. I was also hoping to perfect my execution of some of the more physically challenging yoga asanas, as well as learn to prepare some authentic Indian dishes.

I had seen extreme poverty and disease in Asia and Latin America, and witnessed the degradations of human suffering in slums and shantytowns across the African continent. I knew that many urban centers in India were extremely overcrowded, polluted, and poor, and I was hoping to discover that the rural outskirts of Tiruvannamalai, surrounded by holy land, had been spared that misery.

The nine Holy Ideas or Holy Truths associated with the nine Ennea-gram personality types describe the higher cognitive perspectives that one attains only when truly awake and abiding in non-dual Unity or Christ Consciousness. The Holy Idea is an objective orientation or viewpoint—a particular perception of reality, viewed from the perspective of Essence. In other words, it is an aspect of the God's-eye view of the universe.

The two-hundred-kilometer overland trip from Chennai International Airport to Tiru took four hours by bus. The passing towns and landscapes seemed exotic and familiar—typical of countryside I'd seen in movies and documentaries of southern India.

We arrived in Tiru in the clammy heat of early afternoon. The passengers disembarked and congregated on the shaded side of the bus as the Indian driver methodically retrieved our luggage from the hold. I was watching a bony black cow, standing in the sun, tied to the front post of an ornately decorated Hindu Ganesha shrine. The cow was rhythmically tossing her long tail back and forth, flicking flies off her hindquarters. Her head was down, her flaring nostrils and drooling mouth working together, foraging for food in a slimy pile of old garbage. She wasn't finding anything edible.

Suddenly, unexpectedly, my whole body was convulsed in nausea. I looked up one side of the street and down the other, trying to get my bearings. A strange fear gripped me as I became aware that I was utterly repulsed and horrified by everything around me.

The muddy streets of Tiru were choked with garbage and trash. Discarded plastic bags of every size and color clogged sidewalks, alleys, and ditches, covered vacant lots, piled up around storefronts, and hung hideously from trees and bushes. The humid air reeked of rotting fruit and cow dung. There was a constant, piercing racket of air-horns blaring from dilapidated cars, mopeds, and the three-wheeled auto rickshaws known as *tuk-tuks*. Barefoot children walked in mud and dung and made their way through oily brown slurries covered in yellow foam. Skeletal beggars shuffled around like weary ghosts while homeless women, wrapped in tattered saris, lay like corpses on the ground. My mind rocked and reeled, fiercely judging and rejecting all of it. And then I panicked.

I felt a long, desperate moaning sound of pure anguish leave my body. I closed my eyes and took several deep breaths. I looked around, expecting to be met with offended stares, but the locals were paying no attention, the other bus passengers seemed intent on retrieving their bags, and the bus driver smiled sweetly when he handed me my duffel. I realized it must have been a silent panic. I couldn't remember what had brought me to this place, but I knew something strange and terrible was happening and I needed to go back home. Today. Right now.

> *The Holy Idea is not a concept —it is the total impact of everything that is here, right now. The particular Holy Idea or Holy Truth that can be perceived by the Type One personality is called Holy Perfection.*

I didn't go home that day. I checked into the Lakshmi Guesthouse, a modest, three-story cement building with an open-air lobby in a back alley off Chengam Road, not far from the Sri Ramana ashram. The rest of the day I lay on my narrow bed, alternately sleeping and sobbing, watching the light fade from the oppressively colorless sky and listening to the rusted ceiling fan creak slowly round and round through the heavy air. The next morning I met a small, seasoned group of Westerners staying at the Lakshmi and gladly accepted their invitation to sit with them in silent meditation on the rooftop each day from 6:00 to 8:00 a.m. and 6:00 to 8:00 p.m.

SEVERAL WEEKS PASSED. After morning meditation, I'd walk the surrounding hills and visit the caves where Sri Ramana lived and wrote for sixteen years while becoming enlightened. It was shocking to find that, even here on sacred Arunachala, large expanses of hillside were used as outdoor toilets and the areas around the paths were strewn with garbage and plastic waste. The daily practice I set for myself was to walk in contemplative silence for several hours each afternoon, venturing farther and farther away from the relatively clean, quiet ashrams on the town perimeter, into the dirty, noisy turmoil of the city. I practiced non-resistance: holding myself open and receptive to my experience. I noticed and inquired into my thoughts, feelings, and bodily sensations—while attempting to forego my compulsive self-criticism and judgment.

Most of the time, my mind and body were completely absorbed in resisting the present moment: I resisted the oppressive heat and humidity that kept my dust-covered body and thin cotton clothing saturated with filmy sweat; I flicked and swatted at flies and mosquitoes that had the thankless task of spreading misery and malaria; I stumbled into potholes and tripped over chunks of broken sidewalk, splintered boards, and jagged rocks that bloodied my toes and twisted my ankles. Hiking around in thick brush while trailing a family of Chennai goats, I disturbed the ground nest of a colony of tiny red fire ants. The ferocious six-legged beasts retaliated immediately by flash-swarming up my legs and torso and piercing my flesh with excruciating bites that flamed and stung for days.

During my third week of intermediate yoga instruction at the Arunachala Yoga Centre, I overstretched my thigh and pulled a groin muscle. I endured the intestinal consequences of eating deep-fried samosas sold by street vendors. And I lost my appetite—or my dinner—at the sight of oily, matted rats and rodents scurrying along the floors and counters of the local eateries.

And there were greater affronts to my civilized sense and sensibility. I prayed and wept for the beautiful, bare-limbed children and toddlers who lived around the reservoirs and played in the hazardous waste of the open sewage pits. I had been in Tiru for less than a week before my Type One Reformer self kicked into high gear. It had me devising strategies to recruit volunteers—locals as well as Western visitors—to drain the sewage, clean up the hills, repair the streets, manage the waste, and install portable outdoor toilets in every alley. I made ambitious plans to level and landscape empty lots to provide safe, clean, shaded children's playgrounds in every neighborhood. Clearly I had a lot to do to make this town livable.

Meanwhile, I walked. Every day I walked, one foot in front of the other, farther and farther into my own private heart of darkness. I alternately resisted and surrendered to my habitual reactivity. I wrestled with my intense frustration, examined my personal defects, scrutinized my ulterior

...all of existence has a quality of integrity, goodness, and rightness, just because it is.

motives. I cried and complained, criticized and judged, wept and grieved over my inability to find acceptance and peace.

And then, one muggy afternoon, everything changed—or, rather, nothing changed. I had walked to a densely populated area of the inner city, searching the open market stalls for fresh oranges. After a while, the noise and exhaust of the buses, motorcycles, and *tuk-tuks*, combined with the strong smell of oil and petrol, triggered a throbbing on one side of my head that usually signaled an impending migraine: something I dreaded.

> *The Holy Idea/Holy Truth for Type One is Holy Perfection, which means that, in Presence, we can perceive the unity, goodness, and perfection of this moment, right now. Type One is about the remembrance of Divine Perfection, which is reality seen without the filter of the subjective ego-self.*

Hoping to evade a full-on migraine attack, I left the city market and headed back toward the guesthouse. It was almost four o'clock. By the time I got to my room at the Lakshmi, the water and electricity would have been turned back on for the early evening hours. I looked forward to a cool bucket shower to wash away the dust and sweat. I was walking back along a familiar stretch of road where twenty or so small, cement dwellings surrounded an Olympic-pool-sized pit, filled with sludgy, malodorous water. This is where, over a month ago, I had first seen several little boys pushing homemade wooden boats around the polluted pond. I was alarmed and outraged by the sight of their bare arms and hands bobbing in the putrid brown scum. Was it really too much to ask that The Creator's children have a clean, safe place to play outdoors? I felt a blinding stab of pain behind my eyes that pulsed and flowed around my head like lava.

I took some deep breaths and continued walking. A few yellow-and-black, three-wheeled *tuk-tuks* were going by, transporting passengers in both directions. The sky overhead was its familiar flat, colorless, featureless self; no bright blue patches, no puffy clouds, no golden shafts of sunlight casting purple shadows on the ground.

The long, rutted, brown-gray road and the squat, brown-gray buildings on either side had taken on a similar textural consistency, as though they'd been poured from the same vat of concrete and tar. The small, thatched farmers' huts in the distant fields seemed to be sprouting from the surrounding ashoka trees. The outlines of objects appeared vague and less pronounced than normal.

My focus on the visual stimuli around me shifted to the audio. I could hear my thin rubber flip-flops making cadenced contact with the asphalt and then slapping against the bare soles of my feet. My small canvas backpack, loaded with oranges, was making a slight *ca-choosh-ca-choosh* sound with each step, each shift of my weight.

A *tuk-tuk* driver sounded his air-horn in short staccato bursts as he came up behind me. As the vehicle passed, I heard the metallic wheeze-and-grind of the three-cylinder engine over the quieter, yet distinct, sound of the small, fat rubber tires making squishy contact with the road. Bits of loose gravel, spit out from beneath the tires, pinged against the metal underside of the vehicle. I noticed I was pleasantly surrounded and enveloped by an acoustic symphony of sound.

Two male voices, coming from the *tuk-tuk*, were conversing in Tamil. Something about the ease and intimacy of their melodic conversation allowed me to notice my own sense of uncaused ease and intimacy. I felt a soft, buttery contentment with—well, with everything. The cooling temperature of the moist air, the steady rhythm of my gait, the wide, colorless sky, the sculpted curvature of the earth—it was all part of a single vast and timeless phenomenon, and there was a breathtaking, luminous quality of *suchness* to all and everything.

> When we come to a more transparent state, we see that all of existence has a quality of integrity, goodness, and rightness, just because it is. We truly see, as all the great mystics have told us, that, in the grander scheme of things, everything in the cosmos is unfolding exactly as it needs to.

A dark-skinned Indian woman, who looked to be about my age, was walking toward me, leading a pair of small-horned, floppy-eared goats. She was wearing a brown cotton sari patterned with pink-and-white tropical hibiscus, my favorite flower. My eyes were drawn to the small round red bindi in the center of her forehead. I had learned that the traditional bindi adorns and represents Ajna, the Sixth Chakra, also known as the Third Eye: the eye of spiritual wisdom and knowledge. It also symbolizes a state of enlightenment. In meditation, to enhance concentration, I often focused my inner sight on this very spot between my eyebrows, known as Bhrumadhya. The woman was looking directly at me with the loveliest of smiles. I realized I had been smiling at her approach as well. Something sweet and diffuse shimmered between and around me, the woman, and the two horned goats.

As they passed, I caught sight of a large, orange plastic bag, snagged on the branches of a thorny acacia tree. I tried to decipher the graphics printed on the torn and twisted bag—and that's when I became aware that I didn't mind it. Plastic trash was hanging from the trees, yet I wasn't feeling annoyed or reacting with rage. There was no story running through my mind about the global plague of plastic and consumer waste, no internal commentary on the evil act of littering and defiling Mother Earth. A bright orange bag was hanging from a green acacia on the side of the road beneath a colorless sky.

> *Through Holy Perfection, we recognize the existence of spiritual dimensions in all that exists. Everything is part of the beautiful, grand unity. Everything that occurs is perfect.*

My awareness expanded in waves to include all that I could behold. Ahead in the distance, I could make out the familiar shapes and colors of the Hindu shops and shrines that lined Chengam Road, many of them blessed by the presence of sacred cows standing tied to their posts. Behind me, I heard the melodic sound of children's laughter coming from the vicinity of the reservoir.

The reservoir was not miraculously purified that day. The colorless sky did not deliver rainbows. It was as it was. Everything remained as it had been. Nothing had changed, other than my perspective. I walked on toward whatever lay ahead, looking, listening, sensing, and smiling, wholly intent upon the perfection of the present day.

> *Holy Perfection tells us that, if we're here right now, alive and awake and present, the moment we actually inhabit is always divinely perfect, no matter what is happening, and whatever the color of the sky.* •

Soul Spring

Everything visible has an invisible archetype.
Forms wear down and die. No matter.
The original and the origin do not.

Every fragile beauty, every perfect forgotten sentence,
you grieve their going away, but that is not how it is.
Where they come from never goes dry.
It is an always flowing spring.

Imagine soul as a fountain, a source,
and these visible forms as rivers that build
from an aquifer that is an infinite water.

The moment you come into being here
a ladder, a means of escape, is set up.

First, you are mineral, then plant, then animal.
This much is obvious, surely. You go on
to be a human developing reason and subtle intuitions.

Look at your body, what an intricate beauty
it has grown to be in this dustpit.

And you have yet more travelling to do,
the move into spirit,
where eventually you will be done with this earthplace.
There is an ocean where your drop
becomes a hundred Indian Oceans.

Where Son becomes One. Be sure of two things.
The body grows old,
And your soul stays fresh and young.

—Rumi, translated by Coleman Barks[1]

NOTES

Bonaventure

1 *Bonaventure: The Soul's Journey Into God; The Tree of Life; The Life of St. Francis*, trans. Ewert Cousins (Mahwah, NJ: Paulist Press, 1978), 294.

Perfection as Authenticity and Wholeness

1 Angus Stevenson and Christine A. Lindberg, eds. *New Oxford American Dictionary* (Oxford: Oxford University Press, 2013). Accessed through Apple's Dictionary widget, s.v. "perfect."

2 Ibid., s.v. "complete."

3 Lynn C. Bauman, Cynthia Bourgeault, and Ward J. Bauman, *The Luminous Gospels: Thomas, Mary Magdalene, and Philip* (Telephone, TX: Praxis, 2008), 115, n. 6.

4 Raimon Panikkar, *Christophany: The Fullness of Man*, trans. Alfred DiLascia (Maryknoll, NY: Orbis, 2004), 99.

5 Bauman, Bourgeault, and Bauman, *Luminous Gospels*, 88.

6 Ibid., 117, n. 2.

7 Thomas Keating, *Intimacy with God: An Introduction to Centering Prayer* (New York: Crossroad, 1984), 64.

8 Maurice S. Friedman, *A Dialogue with Hasidic Tales: Hallowing the Everyday* (New York: Insight Books, 1988), 68.

9 Ibid., 66.

10 Panikkar, *Christophany*, xxi.

11 Cynthia Bourgeault and Richard Rohr, *God As Us! The Sacred Feminine and the Sacred Masculine* (Albuquerque, NM: Center for Action and Contemplation, 2011), Disc 2, Track 2.

12 Ibid.

13 Cynthia Bourgeault, *The Meaning of Mary Magdalene: Discovering the Woman at the Heart of Christianity* (Boston: Shambhala, 2010), 55.

14 Bauman, Bourgeault, and Bauman, *Luminous Gospels*, 99.

15 Ibid., 125.

Perfection: A Problem and a Solution

1 John Paul II, *Divini amoris scientia*, sec. 10.

2 Ibid., sec. 11.

3 Thérèse of Lisieux, *Story of a Soul: The Autobiography of St. Thérèse of Lisieux*, trans. John Clarke (Washington, DC: ICS Publications, 1977), 237.

4 Ibid., 223.

5 Ibid., 225.

6 Ibid.

7 Ibid., 226.

8 Ibid.

9 *Collected Letters of Saint Thérèse of Lisieux*, trans. F. J. Sheed (New York: Sheed and Ward, 1949), 303; for an alternate and slightly different translation, see *St. Thérèse of Lisieux General Correspondence*, trans. John Clarke (Washington, DC: ICS Publications, 1982), 1038.

10 *Divini amoris scientia*, sec. 8.

11 Lisieux, *Story of a Soul*, 207.

12 Lisieux, *General Correspondence*, 999.

13 Lisieux, *Story of a Soul*, 224; cf. 2 Corinthians 12:5.

14 Lisieux, *General Correspondence*, 1133.

15 Lisieux, *Story of a Soul*, 188.

16 Ibid., 276.

17 Ibid., 257.

The Messiness of Community: An Invitation to Intimacy, Truth-Telling, and Grace

1 Henri Nouwen, *Reaching Out: The Three Movements of the Spiritual Life* (New York: Image Books, 1975), 24.

2 Richard Foster, *The Celebration of Discipline*, 3rd ed. (San Francisco: HarperSanFrancisco, 1998), 176.

3 Henry Cloud, *Changes That Heal* (Grand Rapids, MI: Zondervan, 2003), 23.

The Way of Imperfection: Teresa of Ávila and Our Blessed Humanness

1 Teresa of Ávila, *The Way of Perfection*, Chapter 32.

2 Ibid, Chapter 28.

3 As spoken in person to the author by Stephen Levine.

4 Qur'an 55:13.

Perfection and the Harmonics of Wholeness

1　Reported by President Barack Obama in his words of public condolence on the death of Nelson Mandela on December 5, 2013.

2　Leonard Cohen, "Anthem," *The Future* (Sony/ATV Music: 1992), compact disc.

3　Richard Rohr, *Yes, And... : Daily Meditations* (Cincinnati: Franciscan Media, 2013), 374.

4　Henri J. M. Nouwen, *The Wounded Healer: Ministry in Contemporary Society* (New York: Doubleday, 1972).

5　Ilia Delio, *The Unbearable Wholeness of Being: God, Evolution, and the Power of Love* (Maryknoll, NY: Orbis, 2013), xxv.

Perfection

1　Scot McKnight, *Sermon on the Mount* (Grand Rapids, MI: Zondervan, 2013), Kindle Loc. 3622.

2　Ibid.

3　Rainer Maria Rilke, *Rilke's Book of Hours: Love Poems to God*, trans. Anita Barrows and Joanna Macy (New York: Riverhead, 1996), 45.

4　McKnight, *Sermon on the Mount*, Kindle Loc. 3642.

The Trap of Perfectionism: Two Needed Vulnerabilities

1　Brené Brown, *Daring Greatly: How the Courage to Be Vulnerable Transforms the Way We Live, Love, Parent, and Lead* (New York: Penguin, 2012), 2.

2　Ibid.

Perfection as an Experience of Presence and Grace

1　Oscar Ichazo, founder of the Arica Institute and developer of the Enneagram of Personality theories, originally assigned the term "anger" to the passion of point One. In my view, anger is too broad and is, in fact, a necessary emotion, whereas this seething, simmering, underlying dissatisfaction feels closer to the experiential core of the One part of everyone.

Soul Spring

1　*Rumi: The Big Red Book: The Great Masterpiece Celebrating Mystical Love and Friendship*, trans. Coleman Barks (New York: HarperOne, 2010), 26.

Center for
Action and
Contemplation

A collision of opposites forms the cross of Christ.
One leads downward preferring the truth of the humble.
The other moves leftward against the grain.
But all are wrapped safely inside a hidden harmony:
One world, God's cosmos, a benevolent universe.